THE NEW SOUTHERN

STYLE

THE INTERIORS OF A LIFESTYLE AND DESIGN MOVEMENT

ALYSSA ROSENHECK

ABRAMS, NEW YORK

TO THE NEW SOUTHERN COMMUNITY,

I WROTE THIS FOR YOU.
AS A THANK-YOU FOR THE DAILY LOVE,
ENERGY, AND WARMTH YOU SEND MY WAY.
THESE PAGES ARE A REMINDER THAT WE
ARE ALL STRONGER TOGETHER, RESPECTING
OUR DIFFERENCES, HONORING OUR CURIOSITIES,
EXPANDING INTO OUR TRUTH, AND
RECLAIMING THE CREATIVE LIGHT THAT
LIVES WITHIN US. THESE PAGES ARE YOURS
AND SO IS A PIECE OF MY HEART.

–

THANK YOU

THE MOVEMENT

INTRODUCTION

Some things in the South are constant. Come-as-you-are hospitality. The sweetest of teas served on wide front porches meant for gathering. Thick drawls and even thicker summer air. Pride in who you are and where you're from.

For a culture whose history runs deeper than its oak trees, these roots of tradition and conviction are strong and lasting.

But some things in the South are *New*. In a place of complicated social norms and dated perspectives, there is a powerful contemporary movement fueled by creative entrepreneurs who are following our passions and taking risks. We're using vulnerability as a catalyst for both creative and personal growth and taking what's beloved, inherent, and honored from our affiliations with the South and making it our own. We are presenting ideas in fresh ways, all the while focusing on unity and acceptance. In turn, the South's creative entrepreneurs are the new tastemakers, bringing a unifying energy to communities who now look to artists and influencers for inspiration, rather than taking cues from society's elite. Though the American South is generally a culture that moves slowly, there is a tangible forward-moving energy. It's starting in the cities and is spreading, breaking free from its guilty past and moving toward the light through creativity, innovation, risk-taking, openness, and a genuine passion to build

upon the best of Southern culture. Women for example, are no longer silent and share a voice that can be heard fighting racism and social injustice. Creatives are also opting for speaking out over silence, projecting bravery and purpose over perfection.

We don't pretend the South has reconciled itself—this is a land that has been built by and taken from enslaved people. We are committed to having the uncomfortable discussions, telling the truth, and letting our curiosity fuel questions, in the name of moving civil liberties, gender equality, and race relations forward. I am merely a photographer and storyteller, but my goal is to shine light on the idea that art and creativity reveal that we are far more alike than different. I am committed to helping change the narrative.

Those of us who subscribe to The New Southern are using our voices as a force for kindness and oneness rather than division and judgment. We are using our craft to change the perception that emotional output is a weakness, to reveal that it is a strength. Ultimately, we're paving the way for the next generation to be freer and more open than those before us, and we are shaping The New Southern minds of the future. We are saying, out with the old formalities and in with the New in our hearts, our minds, our homes, and our businesses, by embracing creative prosperity and community.

MY NEW SOUTHERN

THE ORIGINS, THE SHADOWS, THE LIGHT

THE ORIGINS I am on a plane in my usual window seat, inspired by the clouds moving by me, on the way to photograph another home. I think about light and how without it, you and I wouldn't be here together in this very moment. Gratitude is filling my heart, and I get goosebumps as I think about all the moments that have brought me to this point in my life. Has it been easy? No. But was it all worth it? One hundred percent. I have allowed myself to become obsessed with light, both literally and figuratively. My career as an architectural and interiors photographer is spent following the light as it moves from room to room. Six years ago, I reimagined an antiquated corner of the photography world. I am not your typical photographer. Pioneering a new way of doing business within the industry, I work with clients who are designers and architects to communicate both their brand and expand their digital footprint. With the exposure I create for my clients, I have helped build many small businesses over the years. My camera is my tool, it is the way I communicate with the world, and it was my healing catharsis when I had cancer. But, in order for me to fully step into my light, I had to embrace my shadows. I show up for my creativity daily, which has provided me with a beautiful community and a sense of calling. The images and stories in this book are meant to be thought provoking and inspire stillness in a world that rarely stops to reflect. My hope is to translate what I see through my lens onto these pages, and into your homes and lives. My images are intended to be healing in their calmness and soothing to your eye, and to serve as a reminder that the same light you see on these pages exists within you as well.

—

THE SHADOWS I believe that in life, we learn through our shadows. For me, the lessons began at an early age. When most five-year-olds were learning to ride a bike, my father was teaching me about poker and his bookie (it should be a red flag to any elementary school when the little girl in a giant pink bow wants to be the "house" while playing cards during lunch). The older I got, the more this progressed into much darker shades. It went from sharing innocent poker games that felt like Chutes and Ladders with my dad to witnessing alcohol addiction, knife fights, and how he eventually gambled away any semblance of stability. These shadows taught me everything about my light. Its intensity, its range, its sensitivity, and the distance I would have to travel to be my own hero. I learned how to be my own leader and steady the ship when it storms.

My mother did the best she could as a single mom. She sacrificed for me, showed me strength, and was devoted to shuttling me around Tulsa, and eventually the world, as I trained as a high-level gymnast with my sights set on the Olympics. Then when a freak accident caused me to retire from gymnastics, I quickly pivoted into tennis, despite the financial burden. My mother's investment in my athleticism over the years afforded me the opportunity to go to college—an opportunity I would not have otherwise had—on a full tennis scholarship. I graduated four years later, debt-free and with high honors. I am grateful for these collective circumstances and experiences, and especially for the shadows, because without them, I would have never learned one of the most powerful lessons I still use to this day: With goal setting, visualization, and persistence, I have the power to make anything possible.

After graduation, stability and financial freedom were at the forefront of my mind. I was interested in medicine and dreamed of becoming a surgeon, but the student loans were too risky. I thought the next best thing was to fuse my passion for the clinical environment with business and by working in the medical-device industry. I interviewed with three different companies and none of them would take me without previous corporate experience. So, I got a job answering phones, delivering coffee, and placing newspapers perfectly on all the bosses' leather-topped desks. I showed up every day wearing plastic pearl earrings, brimming with an eagerness to learn, even if it was just an old phone system. I was a secretary to a boutique commercial developer who certainly subscribed to the old Southern idea that women were just meant to sit at welcome desks and look pretty. I was living with two roommates, barely making ends meet, and unable to afford a car. But despite all this, the job allowed me to visualize brighter horizons ahead.

From there, I worked for two *Fortune* 100 companies and continued to be one of the only women in the room. The first job was in industrial manufacturing. I loved the company, and I owe so much of my business acumen to their world-class training program. They had me managing multimillion-dollar territories and moving around the country, and I was soaking up the exposure. I was flying high, gaining

"THE MORE WE ALLOW OURSELVES TO LEAN INTO OUR LIGHT AND CREATIVITY, THE EASIER IT IS TO LEAN INTO OUR CALLING."

valuable experience, and building my 401K. But sometime around 2008, I got a sense that things were changing. Growing up the way I did, I'd developed an incredible sensitivity to my environment that I could tap into when I took the time to listen. At the time, this felt like a secret power. I kept my finger on the pulse, reading all of the business magazines, and paying attention to the tone of my industry, and I developed the distinct sense that manufacturing was shifting. I knew shaky ground when I saw it—I had been living on it my entire life—so I found a new job and resigned a few months before the market crashed and the company I worked for implemented layoffs that would have affected me. I moved back to Nashville for a shiny new medical-consulting job.

There I was, working way beyond Dolly Parton's "9 to 5" with a grueling schedule, but it felt worth it. Most of my days were spent in a refrigerated operating room troubleshooting complex spine cases. My job was focused on solutions, service, and anticipating the needs of those around me. By this point, I was a highly trained work ninja and eager to show my value. I was one of the only women in the country doing what I was doing, and signals from the industry were telling me that femininity was a liability for me in this locker-room environment. I purposely drew attention away from my appearance, which in turn made me feel insecure about my femininity. It was sports bras, baggy scrubs, and little-to-no makeup for me because my goal was to be hired for my knowledge, not the way I looked.

The medical-device industry environment was nothing like the other corporate settings I had been in before. There were more personalities to wrangle and less centralization, and it felt like trying to tame the Wild West. I worked twice as hard and was tested three times as much as my male counterparts. My sole goal was to provide value to the surgeon and his or her staff, and to benefit the patient lying on the table. I always remembered that this was someone's mother or friend, and I was playing a role in helping that person heal.

The surgeons I worked with were kind and taught me as if I were their daughter, and I developed a bond with them. The men in my industry, on the other hand, were threatened by strong women, but I was quietly surpassing them. I was not invited to forge relationships on the golf course or through drinks or handshakes, but I was OK with not being part of this club; instead I made the most of my time in the hospital, and that meant being there from sun-up to sundown.

I kept setting arbitrary goals for myself in order to reach new financial heights. It's clear to me now that the climb was a grasp for freedom and stability, two things that I had never had. I did this for six years, kept my head down, and never took one vacation.

THE LIGHT During one of the largest corporate mergers the company had ever had, I secured an internal transfer to Chicago, but my time there was rife with professional setbacks and financial disappointment. I felt small and alone in the Windy City. Then, two years into my tenure there, my fiancé, Ben (now my husband, who is a head and neck cancer surgeon), noticed a tumor growing from my neck and diagnosed me with thyroid cancer over dinner. We had a long-distance relationship, and the diagnosis was like a big, blaring sign telling me to stop— stop everything, stop fighting for what I thought at the time was "success," stop obsessing over the ladder. From the vantage point cancer provided, my life looked different. I paused and relinquished control. The big, busy world around me became quiet, and everything important came to the forefront, while everything unimportant faded away. I allowed space for myself, connected to my heart, and relied on simple breaths to get me through the day, and from this standstill something extraordinary developed. My stillness spoke to me and I realized that in order to progress, I had to surrender to my discomfort and move toward my fears. When you embrace the shadows within yourself, you strengthen your own light.

Up until then I'd thought that I was fighting for my life—to put food on the table, to keep a roof over my head, and to pay bills. But when I had to find the courage I would need to fight this cancer, I was forced to be honest and admit to not wanting any of the things I'd set out to attain. I didn't want the big new city, the career, or even the condo in which I was living. If I was going to be my own hero, it had to be for something larger than my circumstances and greater than myself. So, I thought I could sell my condo for more than I paid for it, and then use the profit to start a new life, this time only letting my intuition and heart guide me. It was at this point that I did something that unexpectedly would lead me toward my light—I picked up a camera. After reading the manual, I photographed my home in order to list it. Instantly, I fell in love with styling my space and with what I could do with a camera. For the first time in my life, I felt peaceful and connected to myself. I'd asked for a rebirth and found my answer. I heard this whisper telling me to keep taking photos, capturing moments and light, especially in homes where people live most of their lives, creating and loving. I finally understood that while the paychecks I'd received from working in the corporate world made me feel safe, they never made me feel good. I was not truly living, and now, in the most surprising way, cancer was a gift that gave me so much more than it took away. The camera was a tool of connection and brought me to life. I felt like the truest version of myself through this creative outlet. I experienced flow and alignment. I knew that behind the lens was where I was supposed to be. The condo sold in thirteen hours, and I made enough to buy a house in Nashville with Ben and start a new way of living.

—

MY NEW SOUTHERN Today, I have two thriving businesses (my photography business and a branding company aimed to help grow small businesses) and exciting things in the pipeline, and I make my choices based on a vision that allows me to support the people who are working with me. I am committed to bettering the community around me and I allow myself the space to grow, pivot, and be in alignment with my soul. When I discovered my creativity, I became a pioneering voice in my industry and I found my community. I reconciled the hand I was dealt in my past and started betting on myself. I began expressing myself in a way I had never done before. I was putting deep, loving energy out into the world, and it was coming back to me in full force. I started getting messages every day from women saying they were empowered by something I said. I connected with women who were trying to rise above the everyday struggle and reach a new level of living, as well as with women who were hitting milestones within their own cancer recovery. I heard from women who were finally ready to start their own business, go back to school, or enroll in a creative writing course they didn't have the courage, until now, to pursue. Others said that it was because of what I shared that they could take a step back and become more spiritual, and in turn, it made them better mothers, wives, daughters, sisters, and friends. These deep, meaningful connections around the globe allowed me to witness and value our similarities over our differences.

In finding my creative cadence, I tapped into a community of like-minded individuals who shared this crazy, creative compulsion too. I found my place, my home, and my people. I have been hooked ever since. It opened up a whole new world, and I was inspired to put a name to this movement, for you and for the next generation committed to creative prosperity, service, and unity. It's called The New Southern.

THIS BOOK

THE FACES AND PLACES DRIVING
THE MOVEMENT

To make this book, I interviewed creative entrepreneurs from different backgrounds and upbringings, with old and new ties to the South. Some of these makers, designers, artists, chefs, writers, and activists are Southern born, rediscovering their roots and bringing a fresh wave of creativity into their hometowns. Others relocated to the South and are fueling an expansion of diversity and inclusiveness. And some simply lived briefly in the South and made their mark there, later bringing Southernisms with them to other cities around the country.

Some of the questions I ask in the interviews are meant to challenge old beliefs, to get us to start thinking about how we can create a kinder, more empathetic world. I also took into consideration the collective conversations I was having with others, as well as my own experiences of being marginalized in the old South. By starting a dialogue, I believe we can spark progress. The common themes woven throughout the interviews are embracing change, showing up for one's creativity, and using curiosity to deepen communities. The photos are filled with light and beauty, but also you'll find a palpable humanity existing within the four walls of each home. This, to me, is The New Southern.

This project started out as a simple design portfolio. It quickly grew into a story that is less safe, but necessary to tell—a story about celebrating our differences and finding solidarity through creativity. It became important for me to produce more than a style guide or a design book. Yes, I want you to have beautiful, practical takeaways. So I will show you how to incorporate many of the elements that you see throughout the book into your own space. From my thirty-dollar idea to suspend art from your ceiling (page 278), to the rules (and how to break them) for styling the "new mantel"—aka your coffee table (page 312)—my hardworking

tips are presented at the end of each chapter, in sections called Style. But on a deeper note, I also wanted to touch on subjects you wouldn't normally find in a book like this. In this spirit, I have paired my styling advice with sections called Substance. Here you will find my back-to-basics approaches to instill more gratitude, awareness, and stillness in our lives, which I hope will lead us to a more connected version of ourselves.

In the pages to follow, I'm honored to be the first to welcome you into my home, and then you'll discover thirty-one more inspiring interior spaces. Organized by six themes of The New Southern movement, this book was created to encourage you to pursue the things that drive you. You can look for ribbons that tie each chapter together, like the attention paid to geometry in the minimal homes, and the sourcing of natural materials in unexpected ways in the coastal homes, or you can simply return to the book when you need a helping hand of encouragement and inspiration. My intention is for each page to be a respite from the commotion of daily life, offering a moment of self-love and creative contemplation.

By sharing these interviews, I aim to foster a very human experience, one that mirrors the warm feeling of stepping into the homes of Southern creatives, sitting down, and having a meaningful conversation over coffee and biscuits. I want you to hear the inflection in their voices and see the laughter behind their smiles. I want the book to evoke the feeling of looking into another person's eyes with deep understanding. And I want it to leave you with the sensation of having just received a hug or a hot meal, satisfying to the heart and nourishing for the soul. Ultimately though, I hope the people in these pages, and their life stories, inspire you to dream even bigger, bare your authentic core, and embrace your shadows to show the world your brightest light.

BIOGRAPHY
—

FOUNDER OF THE NEW SOUTHERN
ARCHITECTURAL PHOTOGRAPHER
AUTHOR AND SPEAKER
CANCER SURVIVOR

ALYSSA

ROSENHECK

NASHVILLE, TENNESSEE

"LIVING IN THE LIGHT INSPIRES OTHERS TO DO THE SAME."

This journey changed me. I spent almost a year traveling from coast to coast, taking photos, conducting interviews, being fueled by the idea that we are far more similar than different, energized by the creative fabric binding us together. My goal was for the person sitting in front of me to leave a mark on my heart. I was looking for connection and to identify the person's purpose that results from passion. What I received were beautiful, nuanced, and eye-opening responses that transformed me with their insight, awareness, and humor.

I began this book with the idea that there was a creative movement afoot, and I discovered that not only was my hunch accurate, but the shift is far more powerful and palpable than I could have ever anticipated. Asking questions that make you think beyond yourself is as grounding as the grit and soul of the South. I am honored to be the first to answer the questions I asked others that fill the pages that follow, sharing with you my heart and the energy that exists within my home.

This tour of my home will also introduce some common themes that you'll find in the other spaces showcased throughout the book—themes that together embody the New Southern style. For instance, one of the common threads in the Minimal New Southern is simple geometries. In my home, this is reflected in my clean-lined living room accent chair and the artwork above my fireplace from Nashville designer Kayce Hughes. Then there are a few hallmark characteristics of the Laid-back New Southern found in my layering of calming tonal textures, such as wool, hides, linen, mohair, and cotton. Meanwhile, my personal art collection, along with my antique African urns, add a layer of the Collected New Southern. Coastal New Southern touches can be found in the light natural wood floors and industrial marine lighting in the kitchen, while Playful New Southern touches like the colorful Chambers Austelle piece in my dining room add a fun energy to the space. My hope for you, the reader, is that you will be able to cultivate elements from each category in your own space, the way that I do.

—

TNS *Tell us about yourself.* AR I am a light-chasing, intuitive, hardworking, highly sensitive human with a soft spot for the underdog. I have a limitless amount of love to give and a deep connection to the world around me. This has allowed me to be a vulnerable artist, a creative entrepreneur, a cancer survivor, a storyteller, a good listener, and a friend. I also can eat an entire box of Lucky Charms cereal in one day, a newfound skill I discovered while writing this book!

TNS *What ties you to the South?* AR The South is in my blood. Not because I was born and raised here, but because after spending a significant amount of time here, I feel a sense of responsibility to honor a land that was built on the backs of enslaved people. I am not a historian. I am a mere photographer, storyteller, and sparker of curiosity and Nashville was where I found my voice. This is where I became a creative and grew into the woman I am today, and where I continue to find moments inspiring me to be an agent of change. Living in this region demands consciousness, especially as a young Jewish woman. I acknowledge the past along with the current, fraught cultural climate, but I take it upon myself to practice activism through love, creativity, tough conversations, and connectedness. This is how we heal and move toward a healthier system.

RIGHT
A towering six-foot tall Chambers Austelle painting represents a study of liberation versus confinement. The art takes the stage behind the dining table I painted in Farrow & Ball's Strong White.

Leaning art is one of my favorite ways to layer a space. The artwork is from my own personal collection and are gifts from artist friends Josh Young, Michálle Sessions, Erin Clark, and John Shearer.

TNS *What does The New Southern mean to you?* **AR** It is my story and it is anyone's story who has had to dig deep and rely on humility and heart to make something from nothing. The New Southern is a progressive movement, grounded in cultural change, unity, acceptance, love, and creative prosperity in a region of the country that has a contentious, complex, and culpable past. This past can still be felt. So we highlight our similarities, honor our differences, educate ourselves, and support those who are exploring life within the four walls of their home with more creativity, more imagination, more cultural awareness, and more acceptance.

TNS *What inspires you most about the South?* **AR** The determination. The heart. The soul. Most of my family is from New York and my heritage is Italian Catholic from my mother's side and Eastern European Jewish from my father's side. My lineage is a mix of men and women who had to build things from the ground up and persevere in the face of anti-Semitism— workers, makers, artists, and scholars. This resilience is what ties me to the soul of the South and the marginalized groups within Southern communities.

TNS *How do you think creativity unites us across political, social, and economic divides?* **AR** Creativity is synonymous with love and is the light that shines on our oneness, our goodness, our freedom, and our courage. Creativity brings people together in celebrating the arts and developing curiosity about ourselves and those around us. It doesn't matter what side of the fence we stand on or how different our neighbor may be—what matters most is humanizing our differences every day through the lens of creativity, connection, and support.

TNS *How did you approach the design of your space?* **AR** I threw out all the rules, invested in pieces that brought me joy, and took all the time I needed. My husband and I come from very modest backgrounds and are self-made. He put himself through a challenging academic program and I had just resigned from the stability of the corporate world. I was building my businesses during this time and we relied on my savings to furnish the house, which over the years gradually became a calming retreat. I intuitively design our home, letting our rooms represent a future vision that supports stillness and imagination. I love stacks of books, weath-ered accessories, and couches you can snack and take naps on. The ultimate goal with our home is for anyone who walks in to feel a peacefulness that supports our "come as you are" lifestyle. I also love meaningful art, so a very special thank-you to my artist friends—Catherine Erb, Kayce Hughes, Michálle Sessions, Lindsey Grace Whiddon, Angela Allen, John Shearer, Chambers Austelle, Josh Young, Erin Clark, and Angela Simeone, who help bring my walls to life.

"COURAGE IS THE ABILITY TO CONNECT WITH ANOTHER HUMAN AND SHARE OUR TRUTH."

RIGHT
My favorite styling tip is
hiding televisions with art. I
used L-brackets from Home
Depot for the Kayce Hughes
piece. For how to suspend
art from the ceiling like
I did with this Catherine
Erb piece on the far right,
see page 278.

TNS *The secret for creating visual rest?*
AR I witness so much every day that our home is
designed to encourage maximum peace. I have
one paint color throughout the entire house for
continuity. I like for my eye to be able to travel
freely throughout a space. Most of my walls are
intentionally empty. Each room is filled with
neutral tones, including layers of textiles within
the same color family but with alternating
textures (e.g., linens paired with wools and
velvets), and items that evoke serenity and joy.

TNS *Describe your signature aesthetic in
three words.* **AR** Light-filled, intentional, and
approachable.

TNS *The key to making a house a home?*
AR Candy and a comfy couch. On a deeper level,
the key is creativity, intention, and light. We
need less stuff. We need to be more mindful
of consumption—of the items we have in our
spaces, the television we watch, the books we
read, our social media scrolls. Mindful consumption means exposing ourselves to experiences
that facilitate growth and joy, rather than toxic
comparisons. It means leaning into the items
and experiences that empower imagination and
connect us more to one another.

TNS *What are your daily rituals?*
AR I wake up each morning asking myself two
questions: 1. How am I going to show up for
myself today? 2. How am I going to show up for
the world around me?

TNS *What is currently on your nightstand?* **AR** Starburst wrappers, a few hair ties,
and about ten books. Some of these books fuel
my soul—hello, Oprah, Panache Desai, Brené
Brown, Yung Pueblo, and Lalah Delia—and
others are about business and leadership.

TNS *How do you feel when you're creating?* **AR** When I am writing, creating new
content, shooting, styling, and/or developing
new business ideas, I enter a state of flow. Time
stops, there is no worrying, no fear, and I am
connected to the present moment. I feel one
with the world, and it is one of the purest forms
of love I have ever felt. I think creativity begets

creativity, just like love. The more you create, the more you show up, the easier it is to generate more ideas, more moments to fuel your dreams, and more opportunities to help change the world around you.

TNS *How do you let yourself be vulnerable enough to share your creativity?* **AR** I believe life is about connection. One of the most courageous things we can do as humans is to connect with one another on a deeply vulnerable level and share our truth. There was a brief period when we thought my cancer had spread to my lungs, which would have been terminal. I broke down, and the only things keeping me together were my husband's arms wrapped around me. Breaking down broke me open. The only way to live my life is to be connected, free to be myself and creative—and cancer gave me the courage to live this way.

TNS *How do you consider yourself a courageous human?* **AR** Courage is being able to envision a future greater than our present set of circumstances followed by action. I am courageous because I grew beyond an emotionally abusive childhood home. I am courageous because I changed my inner dialogue and now believe in who I am and how I connect with the world. I am courageous because I am always seeking to grow and love regardless of the circumstance. I also kicked cancer's ass and built a few businesses doing so. These are things that scared me, and I did them anyway.

TNS *What life pivots have you had either professionally or emotionally?* **AR** I definitely did not have a charmed upbringing, and cancer was my tipping point. I came out on the other side of it all armed with a newfound license to dream big and to better the world around me. After that, I never asked permission when I had an idea. I was committed to believing in myself and following my gut, and that has been my message ever since—that the only approval you need is your own. I am now intentional with how I am showing up for myself. I had an external event awaken me, but it was my internal intentions that activated a new life and ultimate change. I know this sounds like something intangible to someone who is entirely focused on making ends meet, but I have been there. I get it, and even when you're barely holding on, you can still find a way to connect to the most alive part of yourself and push forward.

TNS *Best life advice you offer, or best life advice you've received?* **AR** Commit to your own creativity and make decisions from a place of love. Simple yet powerful when it is put into daily practice.

TNS *How are you living your best life right now?* **AR** By being present and congruent with my intuition. I strive for internal alignment. This is where my intentions, my thoughts, my words, and my actions are all in harmony. This is a daily practice of mine and what I like to call "living in the light."

LAID-BACK

PART 1

This is relaxed living at its finest. These New Southerners are old souls with fresh ideas. For them, it's all about the roughed up, the patinated, and the unfussy in these perfectly unpolished homes. They prefer comfortable, slouchy couches to staid and formal living room furniture and days on front porches to luxe grandiosity.

The New Southerners featured in the pages that follow often work with their hands and are committed to creating or collecting slow, beautiful things. They're writers and small-shop owners, designers and dreamers. They make business decisions based on heart and intuition as well as pearls of wisdom passed down from loved ones. Their homes, like the family and friends with whom they surround themselves, are crafted from sturdy stock—indestructible and timeworn.

Built on strong foundations, Laid-back New Southern dwellings feature wild greenery, plucked straight from the earth; weathered woods; and native, organic, and gorgeously basic materials, such as linen, cotton, and silk. Carefree yet composed, these informal homes strike just the right chord between folksy and refined. Yet more than anything, these New Southerners know the value in returning to one's roots, in stripping away the unnecessary, setting mindful intentions, and retreating back to nature. This bunch adores the outdoors and a warm mug of chamomile by the fire, and they start the morning with a vinyasa on the back patio. They believe in leather notebooks that get better with time and warm biscuits for breakfast.

They value neighbors and town pride. They built their homes with restored brick from cities worth preserving, and they're staying firmly planted, committed to making the world around them a cozier, more accepting place. They're relaxed and welcoming, and don't mind if you come over and track some mud into the house, because they know those boots have been places and that you're eager for a place to rest. They've been waiting for you, so hang up that threadbare denim jacket, settle into an armchair, and take a deep breath. Then later they'll set you a place at the table, and won't even mind if you stay awhile.

BIOGRAPHY
—
HOST OF HGTV'S *HOME TOWN*
AUTHOR OF *MAKE SOMETHING GOOD TODAY*
INTERIOR DESIGNER

ERIN NAPIER

LAUREL, MISSISSIPPI

Both on her hit HGTV show *Home Town* and in her daily life, Erin Napier reaches out like a true New Southerner, believing that improving one's community is the ultimate act of love and progress. She and her husband, Ben, have made it their mission to breathe new life into old, dilapidated homes in Laurel, Mississippi, through renovation. They invite young families and newcomers to become part of the homespun magic as they transform homes into cozy, hand-crafted spaces with a personalized Southern style. When so many friends and neighbors were leaving their once rundown town for greener grasses and bigger opportunities, Ben and Erin recommitted to blooming where they were planted and living out big dreams in a small town, adopting the philosophy that if you don't like where you live, don't leave it—change it.

—

AR *Tell us about yourself.* EN I'm Ben's wife and still have the wild crush on him that began when I was nineteen. I'm Helen's mother, tenderhearted as raw biscuit dough, an author, a graphic designer, a painter, a musician, a person on television who pretends she is not because it just doesn't seem possible, a homebody with my mama on speed dial, and a connoisseur of grilled cheese sandwiches and other unhealthy buttered foods. I drink Coke in the morning, not coffee, but Joan Didion did too, so I think it's fine. I have some obsessive-compulsive tendencies and don't like when people wear shoes in our house, but I don't ask them not to because I like making other people feel uncomfortable even less! We want to go to Italy, but it stays on the back burner because a long walk around Laurel when the azaleas are blooming is pretty good too.

AR *What ties you to the South?* EN The passing down as people pass on. Grandmother's tea pitcher, the Christmas parade on the first Saturday in December, the cheer at a college football game in the fall. Being sentimental about these things and treating them like talismans is a very Southern thing, I think.

AR *What does The New Southern mean to you?* EN More than a region, I think the word "Southern" has become interchangeable with a specific kind of graciousness and familiarity.

In the South, you'll be called "shug" by a waitress you've never met. Gracious familiarity —it's endearing.

AR *What inspires you most about the South?* EN The grit of it. There's such a mash-up of people and cultures and art and industry in Laurel, where we live, that it's hard to describe it. I can only say it's a glamorous sort of gritty.

AR *How did you approach the design of your space?* EN I'd been keeping an accordion folder of magazine clippings of rooms that inspired me since I was a kid, and my taste never really changed. Since I was old enough to know I loved home design, I've loved cozy Americana, worn wood, linen, slipcovered sofas. So I started making my dream home a real one.

AR *What drew you to your space?* EN I'd loved our house since childhood! I always had my eye on that yellow craftsman cottage on a side street that sits in the shadow of bigger, grander homes.

AR *Describe your coffee table. What's on it, and why?* EN Ben built our coffee table from quartersawn white oak and he turned the spool legs to match the crib he made for Helen. The rack underneath is Helen's secret hiding place for her toys. There is a smudge in the finish on top near the corner where Ben put his feet up after he finished, thinking the polyurethane had finally cured completely. It had not. I wouldn't change it.

AR *What is your secret for layering?* EN I love a warm-brown sisal rug layered with a cobalt blue stripe or a Persian rug with bold reds. I think neutrals shine when they're paired with saturated colors.

AR *How do you create visual rest?* EN Neutral texture like linen, creamy white walls. They always work to water down a room when it starts to feel 100 proof.

AR *What is the key to creating a calm space?* EN Lamp light and music. Django Reinhardt is a good place to start.

AR *What is the New vs. old Southern hospitality?* EN New: potluck. Old: four courses.

AR *How do you achieve ultimate porch love?* EN You need a place to sleep, a lamp, and a candle to keep the bugs away.

"PEOPLE ARE LOOKING TO SEE THEMSELVES IN OTHERS, TO FIND CONNECTION."

AR *How is the Laid-back New Southern reflected in the spaces you create?* **EN** The art may be formal oil paintings, but it's just to dress up the casual outfit the rest of the house is wearing. There's a softness, a rumpled unfussiness, a "take a nap here" coziness.

AR *The key to making a house a home?* **EN** We should let our homes be a little bit weird, like the people who live in them. I wouldn't give up my porcelain Elvis bust for the world, but perhaps that has less to do with style and more to do with being Southern? I wish people wouldn't worry so much about how other people are styling their homes. It removes the individualism, which is what makes home so comforting. You can really be you there, you know?

AR *What is your general home-design philosophy?* **EN** Personal over pretty.

AR *How do you bring that into other areas of your life?* **EN** I want to be genuine in the things I write and share. Not pretty, not perfect. Flaws and quirks are what attract people to your heart.

AR *How does your space support your creativity?* **EN** Our rooms are small with oversize windows that let it feel like we're living in a terrarium when the drapes are open. Sunlight makes you feel more alive. It makes me want to make things. Music, art, biscuits!

AR *How do you let yourself be vulnerable enough to share your creativity?* **EN** I find that the more vulnerable I am with my writing, with what I share on social media, the more it resonates. People are looking to see themselves in others, to find connection. So it's an encouragement to me to share something difficult and see how it helps someone else deal with that same thing in their own life.

AR *What are your daily rituals?* **EN** Every night at bedtime, Ben runs a bath for me with rosemary salts, and every night I am so thankful to have a soaking tub. We renovated our master bath while I was pregnant and filming season two of *Home Town*, and a long bath at the end of the day was the thing I missed the most.

AR *What life pivots have you had either professionally or emotionally?* **EN** When my wedding stationery business slowed and slowed until I realized it wasn't the right place for me anymore, we were in the throes of filming season one of *Home Town* and that was such a gift. It felt like God telling me I was ready to use my creativity in a new way that was outside my comfort zone, out from behind my computer in my quiet studio. It forced me to be brave, while giving me a soft landing.

AR *How are you living your best life right now?* **EN** Having a child puts priorities into focus. I've become very good at saying no to more so I can say yes to time with Helen and Ben. It feels like we're finding that elusive work/life balance people talk about.

RIGHT
Erin loves natural light. Her home features over-size windows with views of surrounding greenery, anchored by meaningful pieces such as the custom kitchen console her husband Ben made.

BIOGRAPHY
—
OWNER OF T.A. LORTON
INTERIOR DESIGNER

TRACY LORTON SALISBURY

TULSA, OKLAHOMA

A true pioneer, Tracy Lorton Salisbury built her home west of Tulsa when there wasn't much there. She found a gorgeous piece of land and erected a house on a hill, positioned at exactly the point at which both sunrise and sunset would be visible in the living room, inviting guests to relish the full splendor of light over the cityscape. With horses meandering around the property and rich earth spreading out for miles, Tracy is living the quiet life in the country. Fashioned from a medley of durable materials, with design elements such as concrete floors and wood chairs in her kid's crafting room, her home was created with the intention of comfortably hosting large groups. Even though she's living on her own slice of the world, away from the hustle and bustle, Tracy still owns one of the most relevant home-design stores in the South, T.A. Lorton. She never believed she could make her mark on design and culture until her mentor and longtime friend Charles Faudree pushed her to believe in herself. Charles is widely known in the design world for his signature French country style, but to Tracy he was simply the man who helped her follow her passion and live her dreams.

—

AR *Tell us about yourself.* **TLS** I am just a girl born and raised in Oklahoma, having spent a little time in Virginia, Kansas, and New York before I settled back in Oklahoma. Once I returned, I followed my heart and opened my home decor shop, T.A. Lorton, without a bit of knowledge of what I was doing. Thirty years later, I could not be more passionate about what I do. Interior design has been my second career, and I have embraced it.

AR *What does The New Southern mean to you?* **TLS** It means being comfortable in your own skin. Speaking and being your true self. Knowing what brings you joy and living your fullest life.

RIGHT
Tracy chose materials for her home to honor wear and tear. Recycled brick floors from Sapulpa, OK, concrete floors, stainless-steel tables, metal frame tubs, and weathered woods are all elements conveying that nothing is too precious and we should focus on creating memories that last.

AR *What inspires you most about the South?* **TLS** It's the people. Beauty in realness is embraced.

AR *How do you think creativity unites us across political, social, and economic divides?* **TLS** Creativity can be about change and showing different points of view and opinions. Exposure to creativity can bring understanding and knowledge. You just have to be open to it. It's about love, kindness, and acceptance.

AR *How do you see creativity as an important force in today's South, and the country as a whole?* **TLS** Creativity is vital. It takes you someplace. It can open your mind. It can show you a different perspective. It facilitates change.

AR *How did you approach the design of your space?* **TLS** The property is just outside of Tulsa, with a beautiful view of the skyline. The surroundings dictated the design, and since it's in the country, we made sure that nothing was too fussy—brick, cement, and reclaimed wood floors are the foundation.

AR *What is your favorite room in your house and why?* **TLS** The kitchen/living/dining room because it's where we gather; it's where we live. The design is casual and relaxed, with continual windows so you feel as if you are living outside. It's about the contrast and mix. Breaking the rules. That's what makes it interesting.

AR *Describe your signature aesthetic in three words.* **TLS** Comfortable, textured, layered.

AR *What is your personal color palette?* **TLS** Blue is at the top of my list. It always seems to sneak into each design, but neutral palettes are a favorite too—browns, whites, ivories, and black. Oh, but then I love pink, and green and yellow.

AR *The key to making a house a home?* **TLS** A home needs places to sit and be used. And layers of lighting—ceiling, table lighting, and wall sconces.

"FAILING CAN BE FABULOUS. I THINK YOU LEARN THE MOST WHEN YOU FAIL."

PREVIOUS SPREAD
Tracy stitched together
two vintage rugs to cover
her large living floor. When
wear and tear occurs, she
uses a blanket stitch with
denim to patchwork the rug,
making it a unique, laid-
back work of art.

AR *What is your secret for layering?*
TLS Layering can feel like stuff unless it is done right. I use the texture of a fuzzy or knit throw, a soft pillow, or loose curtains with trim details. I might also use a large wood bowl, a stack of books, a layering of colors, or a layering of neutrals. Or perhaps smooth marble and shiny faucets set against wood cutting boards and reclaimed wood floors.

AR *What is the New vs. old Southern hospitality?* TLS New Southern hospitality is about family and friends and loving and accepting one another just as we are. It's based in enjoying the differences in each other.

AR *What does creativity mean to you?*
TLS Creativity means listening to myself and being open to hearing and seeing things in a different way, or similar ways but with a new spin to make it all feel fresh again.

AR *How do you let yourself be vulnerable enough to share your creativity?* TLS You just do it. Plow ahead, develop a thick skin, take risks, and incorporate a sense of humor when you fail. Failing can be fabulous. I think you learn the most when you fail. Plenty of times clients have been doubtful about the direction I was going, but I plowed ahead and followed my gut, and was rewarded with awe and joy in the eyes of my surprised clients.

AR *How are you living your best life right now?* TLS By embracing my passion and by not being afraid to step through fear. I have let go (mostly) of the self-doubt. My mind is often telling me, "no, you can't do that," but if I feel it in my gut, and if I can visualize it in my head, I can just break it down into steps and go for it. I close my ears to the doubters, gather those around me who are my cheerleaders, and get to work. I have never been happier, but also can't believe that I am so fortunate to be living a life so fulfilled.

AR *What life pivots have you had either professionally or emotionally?* TLS Two shop moves were small life pivots, but they led me to have confidence to follow my vision and step fully into interior design at age fifty. I took a big life pivot, and grew into who I was supposed to be, and fully stepped up into my potential. And I feel like I am just at the beginning of where I am going! Recently, I had a meeting with a friend who owns a beautiful shopping district in Tulsa, and he was trying to talk me into moving the shop near his district. He told me that women in their fifties are in the most productive years of their lives. I loved hearing that as I was blazing ahead into this second career!

AR *What is your personal mantra?*
TLS Being kind is always something I keep near to my heart. I have had plenty of unpleasant things occur through the years, and, in the end, I am happiest with just being kind as my reaction. I just take unintended outcomes as lessons to learn and choose differently how I engage the next time. You can't control crazy! So just be kind and move on.

AR *Best life advice you offer, or best life advice you've received?* TLS I was lucky enough to have amazing mentors around me through the years. The best advice is that you can be anything you want to be. My mother used to always tell me that as I was growing up. She is as subtle as a sledgehammer. She is the one who called me when I was living in New York City and told me of a cute little spot that was going to be empty in our chic little shopping center back home. I replied, "Mom, I live in New York." She said, "I know, but I just thought you would want to know." I said, "I don't know anything about opening a shop," and she replied, "Tracy, you can do anything you want to do when you put your mind to it." I went home the next weekend and signed a lease. This is the same advice I give to my children, and to any friend who is finding their passion and is scared: You can be anything you want to be. And if it is your passion, it won't feel like work at all.

BIOGRAPHY
—
OWNER OF EMERSON GRACE
FASHION CONSULTANT
BOSS

KIMBERLY LEWIS

NASHVILLE, TENNESSEE

Kimberly Lewis is changing the Nashville fashion landscape and reshaping it for the next generation of courageous women. Her Belgian-inspired boutique, filled with warm woods and soft grays, creates a low-key luxe atmosphere. Locally focused but globally influenced, her handpicked choices for her carefully curated boutique are focused on outfitting and accessorizing confident women of all shapes, sizes, and perspectives. Perhaps this is because Kimberly herself exudes an inner strength that makes others want to be around her, stay awhile, relax, and make moments with her count. Kimberly gives herself permission for reinvention and embraces a "go for it" mentality on a daily basis, while setting an example of these qualities for her daughter. At the end of the day, she is paving the way for the next generation and is a prime example of helping people live their best Laid-back New Southern lives.

—

AR *What ties you to the South?* KL My family, my businesses, and the friends I have developed here.

AR *What does The New Southern mean to you?* KL The integration of people and cultures that have embarked upon the South who may not be from the South, but who have helped to create a change from what the South was "deemed" or pigeonholed into. There is an influx of people coming to this part of the country and a refreshing change of perception.

AR *What inspires you most about the South?* KL The people, which is ironic for me. I came with preconceived notions that I was moving to a place that was backwards, prejudiced, and not accepting of others. I am a very brown girl in a very white part of the country that I wasn't familiar with. I am from Hawaii and California. What I've discovered is that I am in a growing, changing, innovative, entrepreneurial place, reflected in the people, food, arts, and fashion. I am inspired by my personal awareness

and growth around this—there is always going to be a generational shift and I think this is what we are currently seeing here in the South.

AR *What is the New vs. old Southern hospitality?* KL In hospitality, all are welcome. In the old, not everyone was welcome. I feel like the influx of people with a more open mindset and diverse set of experiences is the difference.

AR *What does the Laid-back New Southern mean to you and how is this reflected in the spaces you create?* KL I am a California girl who is pretty laid-back and chill anyway, but I feel the South has a way that makes you take your time to think things through, to think about yourself, and to be more considerate of others.

AR *What is your secret for layering?* KL When it comes to clothing, you need a staple that is transitional. Well before this latest denim trend, I have been wearing jeans—jeans with a heel and a blouse, or jeans, sneakers, and a tee. I think that's how you need to think about life. The people in your life need to be able to layer into everything and every facet. Surround yourself with things you actually love and appreciate.

AR *What is the key to creating a calm space?* KL Surround yourself with the things that give you pleasure and joy. That is where you find your serenity.

AR *How do you think creativity unites us across political, social, and economic divides?* KL I think it's like music. You're a storyteller, and people are going to relate to your story. That is creativity—putting your vision out there, and the people who are attracted to or inspired by or who appreciate your art, they will find you. Art is the unifier.

AR *How do you see creativity as an important force in today's South, and the country as a whole?* KL Because of all the creative entrepreneurs, makers, artists, and singer-songwriters who are moving here, we're really a melting pot like LA and New York, but on a smaller scale.

"WE HAVE ONE LIFE TO LIVE, SO LET'S DO IT."

The people who are moving here are from all walks of life and they are coming from big cities. That big-city vibe is what they like, but they also feel like they can embark on change and influence the diversity and creativity here, and take what being Southern means to them and make it their own.

AR *What does it mean to be a creative individual in the South?* **KL** Taking my personal style and exposing it to others. I think that also includes your vulnerabilities, your truths, and whatever is personal to you. Space, taste, and the ability to say who you are for the people who are attracted to you.

AR *How do you feel when you're creating?* **KL** Fulfilled. Women need an outlet. Whether they are creative or not, women need to know they are doing something that gives passion and joy.

AR *How do you let yourself be vulnerable enough to share your creativity?* **KL** I think it's about having confidence, and that really comes with age and experience. You're able to articulate and communicate more and express more. You've lived life. I know how I am and who I am. Deeply and soulfully. For young girls who have not had the life experience I have had, I would first recommend journaling. When you write your thoughts down, your dreams and your feelings tend to come to fruition.

AR *How are you living your best life right now?* **KL** I am being true to who I am. The older you get, the wiser you become. You learn to listen to yourself more—your body and your thoughts—and you know that there is purpose and meaning in whatever is going on in your head, your mind, and your soul.

AR *How do you consider yourself a courageous human?* **KL** Because I am a risk-taker! I left California to marry my second husband, who is here in Nashville. I pulled my daughter out of a great school. I left an established career. We have one life to live, so let's do it. And it's been really great. My intuition and my gut said that this is what I needed to do.

AR *What life pivots have you had either professionally or emotionally?* **KL** I have been married, divorced, and remarried. I think too many people see divorce as a sad thing. Too many women will stay in a situation because they feel they may not have any other options —whether it's financial or feeling like nobody else will love them. Divorce can be hard, but I am very blessed that I am the product of divorce. Becoming a mother has really been pivotal in my life. Having a child, you learn that life is not really just about you and that you are responsible for another being becoming a good person. I have this strength and deter-mination—I have a drive and a dream. I need people in my life who want to help me make that happen. No naysayers.

ABOVE
The casual-chic boutique focuses on outfitting confident women of all shapes, sizes, and perspectives.

RIGHT
Citizens of Humanity's Distressed Denim Jacket is the ultimate Laid-back New Southern staple.

BIOGRAPHY
—

TAYLOR ANNE INTERIORS
FURNITURE DESIGNER
AVOCADO FARMER
INTERIOR DESIGNER

TAYLOR ANNE BLISS

SANTA BARBARA, CALIFORNIA

Most homeowners would have given in to the temptation to enlarge the 1900s farmhouse Taylor Anne Bliss and her husband bought into the surrounding fifteen acres of avocado trees, but Taylor resisted and left her home the original, intimate size to preserve its character. She opened it up instead by using all the same white throughout the house and showcasing the beams of light that stream in through the windows. She also expanded the outdoor space to include a vintage Airstream and entertaining area so that she could take advantage of the California climate and extend the laid-back, come-and-go feel that her home exudes. Southern touches like her husband's vintage Ralph Lauren original cowboy boots, placed by their farmhouse bed, and butcher block countertops are woven seamlessly with elements of California cool, yet it's the layers of soft material like vintage mohair velvet chairs that lend Taylor's space the ultimate casual elegance. Despite her young age, Taylor has already figured out how not to get caught in the jumble of trend and competition and this confidence is reflected in her home. Hardworking like the folks on the farms that surround her and her husband's cozy cottage, Taylor knows how to face the world with trust in herself, all the while knowing that her warm, welcoming home, like a beacon in the field, will be there to meet her when the day is done.

—

AR *What ties you to the South?* **TAB** My dad has a large family and he was born and raised in Austin, Texas. I spent a lot of time in Texas when I was growing up and we would drive out to my family's cabin on Lake Travis. My grandmother made the best biscuits and gravy using bacon fat, and my grandfather had a barbeque smoker in the back where he would smoke the best brisket. My dad would take me to all the hole-in-the-wall BBQ spots in Austin. Some of my best memories were in Austin.

AR *What does The New Southern mean to you?* **TAB** As a young designer, it is important for me to give my clients something timeless and refined yet a space that also feels vibrant and fresh. When I think of the South I think of deeply rooted Southern values, charm, and hospitality. The South has a grounding nature to it and this sentiment translates to the people too. You can always spot a person from Texas. They are the kindest people. My Southern roots have greatly influenced the way I am.

AR *What inspires you most about the South?* **TAB** The people, the food, and, of course, country music all have a soft spot in my heart. All of these things were introduced to me at a young age.

AR *How do you see creativity as an important force in today's South, and the country as a whole?* **TAB** When you look at the creative landscape, you realize we are all related and each industry affects the other. What is happening in the fashion industry affects the interior design industry and vice versa. Creative industries shape the world we live in—the spaces we spend our time in and the clothes we wear. Creativity is absolutely shaping today's South and sculpting a new path for what we like to call The New Southern. Nashville is a great example of this. It's completely transforming!

AR *How is the Laid-back New Southern reflected in the spaces you create?* **TAB** Our society is much more laid-back than in the past. What I like about The New Southern as far as the design industry goes is that it is honoring our formal past, but bringing it back to life in a new way that feels a little less stuffy.

AR *How did you approach the design of your space?* **TAB** Our home dates back one hundred years. It sits on more than fifteen acres of avocado trees. When we found the home, it was a teardown, but it had so much light and such great potential. I knew it could be a happy home. It's on a farm, so I treated the house as it was—a classic California cottage. We landscaped the exterior with citrus trees, olive trees, and lots of lavender and rosemary. I like to maintain the character of a house, and the space has a cozy, livable feel. With interiors, as in life, if you don't get that instant feeling that a design or piece of furniture works, then it probably doesn't, but there are really no rules for that— you have to feel it in your heart.

LEFT
Views of the surrounding baby avocado trees are visible from the bedroom of this California farmhouse. Bedroom accessories include a Restoration Hardware rug with a Jenni Kayne textured sheepskin.

"THE SOUTH HAS A GROUNDING NATURE TO IT."

AR *What is your favorite room in your house and why?* **TAB** My kitchen. Living on an avocado ranch, you'll always find avocados, and lots of fresh fruits and vegetables from the garden. It has a relaxed feel and gets a ton of use. It's definitely not a "show kitchen."

AR *What is your secret for layering?* **TAB** You really want to mix up textures in a space, with fabrics, baskets, inlaid pieces, plush throws, and different fabrics and materials. If everything is one material, it will fall flat.

AR *What is the key to creating a calm space?* **TAB** Think of a spa—neutral watery colors, plush fabrics, textured wallpaper. You want to feel as though the room is giving you a big hug.

AR *The key to making a house a home?* **TAB** Art and plants breathe life into a space.

AR *What are your daily rituals?* **TAB** My day really begins and ends in my kitchen. At night, a great show with a cup of tea is heaven. I love to lounge on my sofa, drapes pulled, candles lit, with my dog and husband.

AR *What is your personal color palette?* **TAB** I love neutrals, but I design really colorful spaces for my clients. I think keeping my personal space and style neutral and clean helps me creatively. If it were just me at home, everything would be white. White floors, white sofa. My office is all white, which I love, because nothing distracts me. It acts as a blank canvas for me to create others' spaces.

AR *How do you feel when you're creating?* **TAB** Free and inspired.

AR *What does creativity mean to you?* **TAB** It's an opportunity to make the world a better place. Creativity provides a sense of freedom. Zero limitations.

AR *How do you let yourself be vulnerable enough to share your creativity?* **TAB** I think at some point you just have to not care if other people will like it or not and jump in with both feet.

AR *How do you consider yourself a courageous human?* **TAB** I've never played things safe and I'm constantly taking risks. If a project scares me, it usually means it's worth doing. People often ask, "Are you sure you want to do that?" and I think to myself, "High risk, high reward." You have to trust your gut.

AR *What life pivots have you had either professionally or emotionally?* **TAB** When I started my own business, I was lucky enough to get a really big project right off the bat. It was a new-construction, seven-thousand-square-foot, Nantucket-style home in Santa Barbara. It was three years in the making. Every day was uncomfortable for a while. I was trying to communicate interior architectural details with the contractors, and because of my age they had a hard time taking me seriously. They all doubted me, and in the end, they are the ones coming to me saying, "The house looks great, love everything you did, sorry we gave you a hard time." I quickly realized that, even though I was more than twenty years younger than they were, I was actually pushing them out of their comfort zones. This project is now one of my favorites, and because of it I feel confident to take on anything. As Dolly Parton says, "Storms make trees take deeper roots."

AR *What is your personal mantra?* **TAB** Everything happens for a reason, and if it were easy, everyone would do it.

AR *Best life advice you offer, or best life advice you've received?* **TAB** Tomorrow is a new day.

"WHEN YOU LOOK AT THE
CREATIVE LANDSCAPE
YOU REALIZE WE ARE ALL
RELATED AND EACH INDUSTRY
AFFECTS THE OTHER."

BIOGRAPHY

—

COHOST OF *UNSPOKEN* PODCAST

AUTHOR OF *THERE I AM*

SPEAKER

FOREVER STUDENT

RUTHIE LINDSEY

NASHVILLE, TENNESSEE

"CREATIVITY REMINDS US OF OUR
SAMENESS AND OUR CONNECTEDNESS."

LEFT
Ruthie translates the
feelings evoked from her
desert travels into the space
by applying a dusty-pink
sunset hue to the walls of
her bedroom (Farrow &
Ball's Pink Ground).

Walking into Ruthie Lindsey's East Nashville home is a magical experience, like bathing in sunshine. The magic comes not from the "stuff" or decor in her space, but from the healing and cleansing she's done there, and the energy that infuses the world around her as a result. At just seventeen years old, Ruthie was involved in a devastating car accident that left her in chronic pain for years and should have paralyzed her. On the night before her very high-risk surgery, her father, who was on his way to tell her he would sell the family farm to pay for Ruthie's medical care, died in a freak accident after falling down stairs. She couldn't believe the nightmare she was living. After her surgery, she woke up with a different type of chronic pain than the kind she'd had for years before, but one she thought would last forever. She spent her twenties depressed, in bed, and dealing with a crumbling marriage. According to Ruthie, it ended up being one of the best things that ever happened to her. She was living in the depths of shadow and, in order to find the light, realized she had to make a drastic change. She stopped taking all the painkillers she'd been on for years, and a fog lifted to reveal a more incredible, beautiful, and divine world than she'd ever known. Because of what she'd been through, she had a newfound understanding of the sweetness and glory of being alive and now carries that with her every day, inside and outside her home. She embodies The New Southern because she's been able to use her pain to connect with others, through social media, and believes it is her life's mission to help create space to empathize with those living with chronic pain and show them that they deserve healing the way she did.

Awash in natural colors, her home is mixed with family heirlooms like her grandmother's silver and vintage pictures of her beautiful mother, placed in a bowl alongside laid-back boho pillows, sheepskin throws on leather chairs, and modern light fixtures. She is also known for her hats, which are proudly on display on her hat wall, and the Daren Thomas Magee artwork on her door that she'll offhandedly tell visitors represents her in a past life. Driven by wonder and awe at what life can offer, Ruthie showcases this in her home through displaying mementos from her travels, like the animal sculpture from Peru hanging over her bed. Ruthie says that every time she would leave, her late father would say, "I love you, mind your manners, and always look out for the little guy." In a way, Ruthie has taken that as the guiding force of her life, welcoming people into her home with warmth and an almost shamanic wisdom, birthing love out of pain, forging connection out of mutual hope, always looking out for the little guy, and walking alongside that person in glory and grace.

—

AR *Tell us about yourself.* RL I'm a woman with a complex story who has come home to herself. All of my pain and all of my scars have become my roadmaps back to myself. Every painful thing I have ever gone through feels like such a gift, to show me my true north.

AR *What ties you to the South?* RL It's where I was born and the place from which my family hails. I have such a deep love for it, and at the same time feel the weight of its history. I know there is so much pain and suffering and oppression where I grew up, a town built by en-slaved people. I believe we can make conscious decisions to be aware and be different moving forward. It's all about remembering what hap-pened and being intentional, making changes, and being inclusive so that we can make a difference now and for future generations.

AR *What does The New Southern mean to you?* RL A more inclusive, expansive South.

AR *How do you see creativity as an im-portant force in today's South, and the country as a whole?* RL Artistry speaks to the human condition. When you get past all the titles and status and get down to the soul of a person, you see that we are all similar. We struggle, we love, we hurt, we suffer, we overcome, we heal. Creativity reminds us of our sameness and our connectedness.

AR *Describe your signature aesthetic in three words.* RL Welcoming, loving, healing.

AR *What is your favorite room in your house and why?* RL My bedroom. It's my healing space. It has such beautiful energy because I have done such precious healing work on myself in there. I painted the wall above my bed the color of the desert at sunset, one of my favorite settings on the earth, so now I have an extension of it in my room, where I restore and rest.

AR *What is your secret for layering?* RL I love using neutrals and as many different textures as possible, and I love bringing the outside in. I want my home to be an extension of Mother Earth. I also have a lot of old family pieces that are important to me. Everything has a layered story.

AR *What is the key to creating a calm space?* RL Less noise. I don't have a television in my home because it felt like so much noise, and it's an escape I used for so many years to not get quiet and deal with my pain and loss. Now I love to open my windows and hear the birds and watch the sunrise and sunset in quiet, and it feels so serene.

AR *Describe your coffee table. What's on it, and why?* RL It was the last gift my daddy gave me before he died. It's made from wood from my hometown in south Louisiana. I love it so much. I also have a plant and a beautiful rock I found in Santa Fe, and a brass tray with a candle I love. There's also scissors from Australia that I got on a trip, and other knickknacks from my travels.

AR *What does the Laid-back New Southern mean to you and how is this reflected in the spaces you create?* RL There are no rules. Do whatever feels good to you.

AR *What is your personal color palette?* RL Colors I find in nature. I recently painted my front and back doors Pink Ground by Farrow & Ball, which is my favorite paint color. I love to cover myself in rose quartz from head to toe in my meditations and to imagine my energy being protected.

AR *What is currently on your nightstand?* RL An oil diffuser, sage, a candle, my favorite stones and healing oils, basically all the healing aids.

AR *What is the New vs. old Southern hospitality?* RL Freedom versus rules.

AR *What does a home need more of and less of?* RL More love and less of anything that's not coming from a place of love.

AR *What is your general home-design philosophy?* RL I ask, does it make me feel good? Does it feel like it's embracing me?

AR *How do you bring that into other areas of your life?* RL I want my home to feel embracing and healing and I want my energy to feel that way too. I aim to carry that with me wherever I go.

AR *What are your daily rituals?* RL I wake up very early. I do twenty minutes of shadow work journaling and then thirty minutes to an hour of mediation. If I have time, I also love to read, and do yoga. I have about a two-hour routine that I try to complete each morning, and it starts my day off so beautifully.

AR *How does your home help you with those rituals?* RL I have my room set up in such a beautiful way that aids me in all of my healing practices, and if it's nice out I love to do those things in my backyard.

AR *How are you living your best life right now?* RL Being my truest, wholehearted self. Loving exactly who I was created to be.

AR *Best life advice you offer, or best life advice you've received?* RL You are the love you are looking for.

RIGHT
Hat walls are a tried-and-true New Southern design technique. To achieve this laid-back look, I recommend brands such as Stetson, Lack of Color, and Janessa Leoné.

OVERLEAF
Mixing old and new, Ruthie pairs family heirlooms and vintage photographs of her mother with modern lighting fixtures and sheepskin throws on leather chairs.

BIOGRAPHY
—
AUTHOR
HOST OF *HEY, GIRL* PODCAST
WELLNESS CONSULTANT

ALEXANDRA ELLE

GERMANTOWN, MARYLAND

Entering Alex Elle's house feels like a warm embrace. The combination of soothing grays, warm woods, and brass accents, along with the energy of her family, makes her space a calming, relaxed refuge from the world. Meanwhile, details like the salt bottle branded with her daughter's name, Isla, are prominently displayed to lend a deeply personal feel. It is these small moments, like the tobacco-colored worn leather journal in her bedroom, that create visual interest as well as a laid-back, lived-in vibe. Even though the family only recently moved in, it is easy to see how they'll dig deeper into this nest, forming layers over time, making it more and more their own.

—

AR *Tell us about yourself.* **AE** I became a mother at eighteen in a very unideal situation, but I decided that I was going to be the mother I didn't have and love the way I wasn't loved. It was time for me to change. I was on a really dark path and I didn't want my darkness to be contagious to my daughter. This was my first shift. My second shift was around twenty-two, when I made the decision to invest in myself. This meant letting go of friendships not serving me. I let go of being undervalued in my job. I worked at a nonprofit in DC and no one cared about my thoughts or what I had to offer—and I wasn't even sure what that was yet, but I wasn't going to find out if I stayed there. I then met my husband, at twenty-three, when my first book was out, and it was a bestseller. Now I am twenty-nine years old and a homeowner and I get to stay at home with my kids, and my husband can quit his job if he wanted. I had to choose myself because I wanted to be a better person, a better woman, and ultimately a better mother.

AR *What ties you to the South?* **AE** My Nana's people are from Red Oak, Virginia. I remember going there during the summers as a little girl and it being dirt and gravel roads and my family members living on the same plot of land. The kids would run around from house to house. My Nana is really strong, resilient, and kind and has always held her own because she has had to.

RIGHT
Soothing grays, warm woods, and brass accents create a calming atmosphere in Alex's home, accompanied by tabletop accessories from Target.

AR *What does The New Southern mean to you?* **AE** If I had to place a word on The New Southern movement, it would be community. Community serves us by helping us see and understand the beautiful and unique differences of the people around us. Community shows me how to lean deeper into compassion, understanding, and empathy for others. Part of how I serve my community is similar to The New Southern, as I am offering spaces and platforms specifically for women to showcase their skills and talents and tap into their inner voice.

AR *What inspires you most about the South?* **AE** I have to say the food, for sure, and also the faith. My Nana is rooted in faith and she tells me that I have the life I have because she prayed for me. I think this is really special. Although I am not particularly religious, I admire my elders who have that faith in something greater than themselves, something they feel guides their lives and the lives of their loved ones.

AR *How do you think creativity unites us across political, social, and economic divides?* **AE** I think creativity gives people space to breathe and to learn what they're capable of— be it from observing someone else's creative force or from leaning into their own creativity. I think this is really important because art translates in so many different ways. As an artist, I feel connected to photographers, painters, calligraphy artists, and spoken-word poets. There are so many voices and outlets for creativity, and I think it encourages people to stop and inhale—or maybe say, "I don't understand that, but look how it is making me think about something differently."

AR *How are you living your best life right now?* **AE** Something coming up for me lately is "things being OK," even though I have so much on my plate. I'm giving myself permission to enjoy what life is affording me, and what my hard work is affording me, and what I am able to do for my family and my children, knowing that at the core of my being I am happy. Sometimes I feel guilty about this because there is so much suffering in the world, but I still give myself

"SHOW UP, DON'T SHRINK, AND BE BIG."

LEFT
Creating spaces to write, dream, and reflect are important to Alex and her family. The bedroom includes a worn-leather journal for soulful thoughts.

OVERLEAF
The studio features floating CB2 bookshelves and an inspirational pennant by Rayo & Honey.

permission to be rooted in joy. I'm finding that balance and harmony between being concerned about the world and leaning into my gratitude.

AR *How did you approach the design of your space?* **AE** I love mixing metals like brass with warmer wood tones. Our space is very neutral, timeless, and we can add pops of color here or there with plants and art, but for the most part I like to keep things in a calming palette with creams and grays. I believe in investment pieces that last a lifetime and we can pass down to our children.

AR *How do you consider yourself a courageous human?* **AE** I am not a big risk-taker. When I initially think of courage, I think of taking a risk, but when I pull back the layers a little bit more, it's doing the thing that is uncomfortable. Facing the hard things is courageous.

AR *What is your personal color palette?* **AE** I love gradations of creams, blushes, and grays, and pulling in some contrast with olive green.

AR *The key to making a house a home?* **AE** I feel like love is so cliché, but it is so true. Love and laugher are the foundations of our home. I was so excited to move into this house because we finally have a dining room table and we can all sit at the table together.

AR *What are your daily rituals?* **AE** My daily ritual is having a cup of French press coffee, or as of late having a cup of ceremonial cacao, which is planted and harvested in a really intentional way. You brew it it at a specific temperature and you inhale steam from the cacao—it is a moving meditation and all about the intention.

AR *How does your space support your creativity?* **AE** Our space supports me by offering a lot of natural light in our living area because I do most of my work in the living room.

AR *How do you feel when you're creating?* **AE** I am going to be really honest—because I am a mother and things are hectic, lately I feel rushed—rushing against Isla's naps, or rushing against a phone call, or what have you. When I work, I need absolute quiet. I can't listen to music with lyrics or anything, so what I have been trying to do is take some moments when I am in my flow to prepare for interruption, be OK with it, and not beat myself up about it.

AR *Best life advice you offer, or best life advice you've received?* **AE** Something that I have been talking about with a friend for the past year has been celebrating our suffering and not hiding from it. Finding ways to soothe the suffering, which in turn makes space for self-care and self-actualization and awareness. I think we live in a world where, as women, we're supposed to be social media perfect, and the real test of self-love and self-care comes from understanding that suffering is a part of life and loving ourselves through that suffering. It should be acknowledged and celebrated in a way that is realistic.

AR *What life pivots have you had either professionally or emotionally?* **AE** My mother and I have always had a tumultuous relationship, and with boundaries it is easier now. There was also a time when no one encouraged or believed in my writing. No one but me and my husband thought I could do it. Then my boss called me a low-budget employee and told me not to forget my place. Up until then I'd been afraid to fly or fail. I was stuck, and after he said that, I just quit on the spot. Two weeks after that, I got my first speaking job, at Ohio University, and I have been flying ever since. I didn't know what self-care was or self-choosing was, and I didn't know what saying "yes" to myself meant, but I do now.

AR *How do you create visual rest?* **AE** Our neutral color palette and keeping things minimal help me to think clearly and not overdo it. I am easily overwhelmed and I want our house to be a place of peace, beauty, and relaxation.

AR *What is the New vs. old Southern hospitality?* **AE** New Southern is lavender lemonade with a sugar rim and old Southern is sweet tea that is too sweet.

AR *What are some of your favorite affirmations?* **AE** Show up, don't shrink, and be big—this is the biggest one I have to tell myself every day.

BIOGRAPHY

—

COFOUNDER OF MCGEE & CO
COFOUNDER OF STUDIO MCGEE
AUTHOR
INTERIOR DESIGNER

SHEA MCGEE

PARK CITY, UTAH

"I CAN DO HARD THINGS . . . IT'S WHAT I TELL MYSELF EVERY SINGLE DAY."

They say you're only as strong as those you surround yourself with, and Shea McGee understands that sentiment perfectly. Standing in the brand-new office space for her team of seventy-six (mostly women), who help complete the day-to-day work of running the design empire she and her husband, Syd, have built, she is enveloped in the positive energy, excitement, and unwavering dedication of her creative crew. The Houston native has been heading up a multidimensional design studio complete with a world-class online presence and a large-scope product line for many years now, but this is the first glimpse of the work space behind the magic. A wizard at imbuing her spaces with warmth and personal touches, yet still keeping things light and airy, she puts her signature style on prominent display with woven-basket light fixtures over the kitchenette, coupled with bright whites and light-wood elements. She has translated her Southern roots into an approachable, relaxed style mix anyone can incorporate—a clean aesthetic with a touch of farmhouse. But nowhere is her warm, active role more apparent than in her job being a mom of two, showing how you can be there to pick your children up at school and still level up on your career, and yourself, every day.

—

AR *What ties you to the South?* SM My family moved to Houston, Texas, two weeks after I was born, and I was raised there.

AR *What does The New Southern mean to you?* SM To me, The New Southern isn't about tradition; it's a frame of mind. The New Southern is about finding beauty in the everyday and embracing a life filled with love and substance.

AR *What inspires you most about the South?* SM I'm an interior designer and there are few things more inspiring to me than driving through tree-lined streets filled with charming Southern homes. From the limestone and brick to the boxwoods and copper lanterns, the style stands the test of time.

AR *How do you think creativity unites us across political, social, and economic divides?* SM Whether we're in boots or heels, we can all find ourselves tapping our toes to the beat of the same song. I love that creativity speaks to the mind and heart in ways that transcend time, money, and point of view.

AR *How do you see creativity as an important force in today's South, and the country as a whole?* SM I've had the opportunity to share creativity in the design space with millions across the country—it has connected me with others who share the same passion for finding beauty in the everyday. I view creativity as a way to connect, live, and bring joy to each other. I think that wherever we live, we could all use a little more of it in our lives.

AR *What does it mean to be a creative individual in the South?* SM Although I no longer live in the South, I think it means that you are part of a community of creatives that is forward-thinking while still honoring your roots.

AR *How did you approach the design of your space?* SM We moved our office into this new studio about six months ago. We were bursting at the seams and needed more space to create and accomplish big things. My surroundings have a huge impact on the way I feel, and that greatly affects my flow of inspiration.

AR *What is your general home-design philosophy? How do you bring that into other areas of your life?* SM I am known for clean-yet-collected laid-back style that mixes styles, eras,

and price points. I believe my style evolved as a result of loving so many different styles that I needed to find a way to put them together in a beautiful and livable way. It is authentic to me and I hope to live this way in all areas of my life. What I love about design is that when we create environments that inspire us, we tend to spend more time in them, because they make us feel good. I think we feel best when we're comfortable in our own skin and living an authentic life.

AR *Describe your signature aesthetic in three words.* **SM** Light, clean, collected.

AR *What is your favorite room in your house and why?* **SM** The kitchen, because it's where we spend the most time as a family. I pray my girls never forget sitting on our countertops baking cookies together on a Sunday afternoon.

AR *Describe your coffee table. What's on it, and why?* **SM** My girls are six and three. We have a huge basket under the table to hide a few books and toys, and on the table a few coffee-table books with some replaceable objects!

AR *What does the Laid-back New Southern mean to you and how is this reflected in the spaces you create?* **SM** It is all about approachability and livable spaces that are rooted in the classics. When I design spaces, I start with clean, classic pieces that will stand the test of time and make people want to sit and stay awhile.

AR *What is your secret for layering?* **SM** Vary your textures for the greatest impact. Think chunky throws paired with Belgian linen.

AR *How do you create visual rest?* **SM** Neutral and natural things are what give us a moment to breathe between colors and patterns.

AR *What is the key to creating a calm space?* **SM** Muted colors and natural light.

LEFT
Natural light and mountain views keep the team inspired in the main office work space, featuring IKEA desks and Circa Lighting's Goodman pendants designed by Thomas O'Brien.

AR *What is the New vs. old Southern hospitality?* SM To me Southern hospitality is a bit stuffy and very overdressed. The New Southern is about authenticity and creating environments that are inviting and speak for themselves.

AR *How do you achieve ultimate porch love?* SM A swing, layered doormats, a grouping of beautiful planters, and a lush wreath.

AR *The key to making a house a home?* SM Layering. Layers of texture, personality, and style add up to a home that tells a story and creates a comfortable atmosphere. Before adding the layers, I like to strip spaces down to the essentials and add back in only the pieces that meet both form and function.

AR *How does your space support your creativity?* SM It's all about the natural light. Light is the most inspiring gift I can give myself. At home and the office, we have windows that support that.

AR *What does creativity mean to you?* SM To me, creativity is reaching within, listening to your instincts and then making, doing, and producing.

AR *How do you feel when you're creating?* SM When I'm creating, I get tunnel vision. I look at each project like a puzzle that needs solving and I stay in the zone until it feels right. I think, dream, and talk about design incessantly.

AR *How do you let yourself be vulnerable enough to share your creativity?* SM At a certain point, I think I just had to get over being nervous. A lot of it had to do with forming a habit of putting myself out there. I have put in so many hours of developing my design experience that I finally feel confident enough in my abilities to know that even if someone doesn't like what I'm sharing I'm still a talented designer.

AR *What life pivots have you had either professionally or emotionally?* SM My degree is not in design. I studied communications and got my start in public relations, but I had this interest in design that I just couldn't shake, and with some coaxing from my husband, I took the plunge into a different field. I have had to learn on the job and use each mistake as a learning opportunity. This has shaped who I am as a designer and a person, because I no longer see things I've never tried as impossible.

AR *What is your personal mantra?* SM Stay close to the sunshine. I want to be a light to others and I want to be surrounded by people who share that point of view.

AR *How are you living your best life right now?* SM I have been able to turn my passion into a career that inspires others to make their homes more inspiring places to be. This dream has come to fruition while creating a life that allows me to spend a lot of time with my family.

AR *Best life advice you offer, or best life advice you've received?* SM I can do hard things. It's what I tell my two daughters and it's what I tell myself every single day.

ABOVE
Unframed oil paintings add warmth to the light and airy space.

RIGHT
The kitchenette welcomes you when walking into the work space with thoughtful details such as oversize rattan pendants and warm woods.

THE BAR CART IS
THE NEW CHINA CABINET

STYLE

PREP TIME: 10 MINUTES
BAR CART

YOU WILL NEED
—

MAGNESIUM BATH FLAKES

CLARY COLLECTION BATH
  AND BODY OIL

SEEDED EUCALYPTUS

WHITE SAGE

SELENITE CRYSTALS

CLARY COLLECTION
  CALENDULA FLOWER SOAP

CONCRETE PLATTER

CB2 GO-CART IN WHITE

China cabinets were once a mainstay in Southern homes, but their formality and fussiness don't fit into The New Southern way. They locked away objects that were typically relegated to special occasions to impress distant relatives, meant to be seen and not touched. By contrast, The New Southern embraces daily, casual engagement with things we love, and it is this relaxed vibe that has allowed for the reemergence of the celebrated bar cart in new and exciting ways. Allowing for room to play, bar carts are a great focal point with broad appeal. They can be styled with family heirlooms or simply with a floral arrangement and a few inexpensive flea market finds. Mostly though, they're a chance to showcase your personality, and not be confined to the wedding pattern your great-grandmother picked decades ago. Bar carts are meant to engage your guests with a laid-back, serve-yourself attitude, and they don't even have to be stocked with alcohol. Here, I've adapted the bar cart into a bath cart that promotes soothing vibes and tranquility for a personal tub moment we can all enjoy.

EVENING RITUALS
ARE THE NEW NIGHTCAP

SUBSTANCE

This bath cart brings with it a cleansing energy. It invites a daily practice to quiet the mind and create a space where we can decompress each night and create pause, because power lies in the capacity to hold space for ourselves and be still. Stillness speaks. Plus, water is such an energizing force in my life and a deep conduit of inspiration. Tub time is a personal evening practice of mine, and I am honored to share such a life-giving ritual with you. It helps me stay focused, generate creative energy, connect to my heart, and ensure I am making decisions from a place of love. Centering myself using water, pause, and breath, and having the items to create this experience readily available, manifests energy clearing, healing, and renewal.

—

HOW TO PREPARE: Run a warm bath with two handfuls of magnesium flakes and Clary Collection bath oils. Light the sage (also lighting candles is optional). Get into the bath and close your eyes. Start focusing on your breath. With each inhale, focus on breathing in pure white light and love. Imagine your life source. (Hint: Think of a time in your life that you connected to nature in an energizing way, when you were in awe of, or transfixed by, its magnitude. My life source is driving up the Pacific Coast Highway, with the ocean on my left and cliffs on my right.)

Start visualizing this energy entering the back of your head, feeling it behind your eyes, releasing tension, and moving down your neck and through your chest, into your tummy, along your arms, and out to your fingertips. Let the white light run down your legs all the way out through your toes. Visualize this energy moving throughout your entire body. With each inhale, focus on breathing in cleansing, purifying air filled with white light, and then breathe out all the things that no longer serve you, or are negative, even an unwelcome outcome. Do this a total of six times. This helps clear the day. Now you can dream, feel the feelings attached to your deepest passions, and continue to innovate. Soak in peace. Soak in stillness. Soak with deep love.

COASTAL

PART 2

Coastal is not just a geographic location—it's a mindset. Delicate breezes, tangled beach hair, and sunset cocktails are all part of the coastal lifestyle. Every weekend is a staycation for the folks in this category because most of the homes showcased here are their primary residences. While the image of coastal Southern homes might conjure thoughts of navy stripes, anchors, and seashells, The New Southern takes a less-expected route, one that is all about elegance and drama.

The homes featured in this category make intentional use of white to reflect the sun streaming in through wide windows and employ Lucite for modern airiness and functionality, which are both hallmarks of the Coastal New Southern. They evoke the ocean through unexpected use of the color blue in different tones, from electric to cornflower, instead of the traditional navy. Nods to the nautical come in the form of submarine-metal kitchens and ship-like staircases, and driftwood appears in theatrical and unexpected design elements, from large sculptural pieces to raw wood bannisters. Instead of patterned fabric, you'll find tortoise shells or other unpredictable uses of texture in uses of texture in these homes, as well as a worldly feeling of culture and travel. These sophisticated beach dwellers hail from both the East and West Coasts and allow us a sweeping look at their varied styles. They're hardworking entrepreneurs during the week, running high-energy businesses and overseeing important decisions, but on the weekend, they use their homes to unwind. They slip into sandals and flowy cotton clothes and take the time to walk on the beach and get centered. They're spiritually connected souls who know how to enjoy the small moments. So come along, put your bare feet in the sand, and let's watch the waves gently lap the shore together.

BIOGRAPHY
—
FINE ART PHOTOGRAPHER
NEW YORK TIMES BESTSELLING AUTHOR
TRAVELER

GRAY MALIN

LOS ANGELES, CALIFORNIA

"I THINK EVERYONE ULTIMATELY APPRECIATES WHEN SOMEONE BRINGS SOMETHING NEW TO THE TABLE."

There is no greater place to view Gray Malin's photography than in his own home. To see how the world-renowned photographer seamlessly weaves his iconic coastal aerial shots intimately into his New Southern decor is a truly fun experience. With a design sense fostered by his mother (a former shelter magazine editor), Gray takes traditional concepts and infuses them with his own signature style. For this space, he worked with Homepolish and Sloane & Studio Interiors, and they used layered rugs, blue wallpaper, and rattan to conjure a coastal vibe, but they chose modern dotted patterns paired with unexpected powder blue lighting fixtures for a touch of modern whimsy. Though neat and tailored, the space is also peppered with family photos, which makes it feel cozy and personal. A consummate professional in every sense, Gray Malin not only creates stunning work, but he also has pioneered a new way of living and working as a fine art photographer. With books, home and travel accessories, and prints to his name, he makes his work accessible to all, and transports viewers to exciting locales the world over through his art.

—

AR *Tell us about yourself.* **GM** I am a son, brother, husband, father, and entrepreneur who has created a life driven by the innate need to create artwork that sparks joy in its viewer. I value family and friends above everything else and am thankful every day for the love and support I've been given, as I know I am who I am today because of it. I am a true optimist and always try to see the beauty in life, whether it's something as simple as fresh flowers or an awe-inspiring, breathtaking coastline.

AR *What ties you to the South?* **GM** I grew up in Dallas, Texas, which some people would argue is an entity in itself, rather than simply being part of the South. Considering the sheer size of the state, I don't necessarily disagree, as it certainly has its own idiosyncrasies that are perhaps best understood by a Texan.

AR *What does The New Southern mean to you?* **GM** A generation of Southerners who value tradition yet are dismissive of notions that are simply unfounded, out of touch, or irrelevant. They embrace the opportunity to meet new people, and explore destinations near and far, all the while with a smile on their face and well-mannered appreciation in their voice.

AR *What inspires you most about the South?* **GM** I am drawn to the traditional architecture seen in various parts of the South. In fact, I would say my home in Los Angeles has a Southern appeal, which is why I was drawn to it.

AR *How do you think creativity unites us across political, social, and economic divides?* **GM** I think everyone ultimately appreciates when someone brings something new to the table. We all want to be intrigued and that's what creativity does for us all.

AR *What drew you to your space?* **GM** The classic Southern exterior architecture with large white columns and a front porch combined with the light, airy, and open California contemporary interior floor plan.

AR *How did you approach the design of your space?* **GM** I like to begin with the artwork in a room then build around it.

AR *Describe your signature aesthetic in three words.* **GM** Unique, classic, and inviting.

LEFT
Gray's "Portofino Vista
Triptych" takes pride of
place in this bedroom
inspired by his coastal
travels.

OVERLEAF
The woven-rattan Serena
& Lily twin beds in the
guest room complement
the coastal hues throughout
Gray's home.

AR *What is your favorite room in your house and why?* **GM** I love our master bathroom. It calms me before I go to bed and it soothes me when I wake up.

AR *What is your favorite light paint color and what is your favorite dark paint color?* **GM** I love a pale, pale pink, almost peach color. Then for dark, a rich slate gray is always aesthetically pleasing.

AR *What is your general home-design philosophy?* **GM** It's on par with my lifestyle brand's motto, which is to Make Every Day a Getaway™. The work I create is intended to inspire joy and transport you to your happy place, so that very much applies to how I design my home.

AR *How do you feel when you're creating?* **GM** Invigorated, overwhelmed, excited, challenged, happy, nervous, ecstatic—all of these things and more!

AR *How do you consider yourself a courageous human?* **GM** When I set my mind to something, I am very tenacious about accomplishing whatever it may be, regardless of who tells me no or that it can't be done. I think that's my most courageous trait.

AR *Living by the water allows a certain sense of calmness. How do you implement that calm in your daily routine?* **GM** Working out, even if for a quick run, is imperative to my health. Exerting that energy helps clear my mind and helps me approach the day with a confident calmness.

"I VALUE FAMILY AND FRIENDS ABOVE EVERYTHING ELSE AND AM THANKFUL EVERY DAY FOR THE LOVE AND SUPPORT I'VE BEEN GIVEN."

BIOGRAPHY

—

RAQUEL GARCIA DESIGN
JEWELRY DESIGNER
INTERIOR DESIGNER

RAQUEL
GARCIA

FAIRFIELD, CONNECTICUT

Raquel Garcia looks like she just came in from the beach, complete with air-dried hair and a peaceful, breezy way about her. The concept of coastal living is woven into every aspect of her life in Connecticut, from the way she embraces the outdoors to the way she meditates by the sea to create alignment for herself. But don't let the white jeans fool you—Raquel is every bit a sophisticated designer, working in the city often with high-end clients or taking meetings for her recently launched jewelry line. Her home is such a bastion of lightness and serenity, it almost feels as if it's floating. Glass elements like her coffee table and bannister coupled with stunning whitewashed floors reminiscent of driftwood give it an ethereal quality, while the high-gloss white lacquer shiplap makes it the quintessential Coastal New Southern space. Then there are the communal spots like the kitchen bench and banquet that speak to how important family meal time and togetherness is for Raquel. Fueled by a strong Latin influence and the strength of the women in her family, she was determined to create a home that is not only beautiful but feels connected to her three daughters.

—

AR *Tell us about yourself.* **RG** Oftentimes others see us better than we see ourselves, and I've been told that I am very courageous and brave, generous and kind, and very passionate and caring.

AR *What does The New Southern mean to you?* **RG** A fresh and vibrant way of taking old classics and using them in your everyday lifestyle—for instance, maybe it's a sterling cup that would've been stored in an old cabinet but you now use as a pencil holder on your desk— which is how I love to design.

AR *What inspires you most about the South?* **RG** The charm, the culture, and the etiquette. People are warm and friendly, still using manners, and there's a sense of charm.

AR *How do you think creativity unites us across political, social, and economic divides?* **RG** Creativity is a universal language that brings people together that normally wouldn't find each other. Creative people don't think linearly; if you're creative, you think broadly, and I think that's the common bond.

AR *How do you see creativity as an important force in today's South, and the country as a whole?* **RG** I see creativity inspired in the South being more in tune with nature and more communal. I personally love all the amazing artists coming from this region that are painting the most ethereal art that highly inspires me.

AR *What does the Coastal New Southern mean to you and how is this reflected in your home?* **RG** It means living with beautiful, classic things in your home but not keeping them in a precious way, instead actually using them in practical ways. For example, the pieces from our grandmothers don't have to be stored away, but can be used daily—like beautiful tablecloths and silver trays for a Sunday brunch or weeknight dinner, and candlesticks in the home for daily use, rather than just once a year. I love to use my mother's sterling silver in my everyday cabinet of forks and knives.

AR *What drew you to your space?* **RG** The natural light I could create in the home because the backyard is facing west is what drew me. The house felt bright, but also private within the beach community. I approached the design of my space by moving with the natural flow

"CREATIVITY IS A UNIVERSAL LANGUAGE."

with the western light and creating openings and spaces with windows and doors.

AR *Describe your coffee table. What's on it, and why?* RG My coffee table is made of acrylic, glass, and brass and it's from the early 1940s; it's French and I love it because it's vintage and imperfect and reflects my signature aesthetic. It has a glass drawer with my favorite things right now—seashells from a family vacation, a favorite book opened to view easily. I love the personal feel to it, being glass and open to view.

AR *The key to making a house a home?* RG A home needs more areas that bring a family together, whether it's the dining room, kitchen, or even the bedrooms. Each of the pieces of furniture can create connection, whether it's an oversize bed for your child where you can read them stories comfortably, or a cozy bench in the kitchen or dining area so everyone is able to linger. In the family room, there can be pouf seating so you can come and go as you need to—if you're making all the food, you're able to pop in and out of the seating area and join in on a fun part of a conversation while you're still cooking.

AR *What is currently on your night-stand?* RG Every calming element that you can purchase—my Bible, my journal, my water, lavender, topical CBD rub, natural vetiver essential oil from a woman in Haiti, a natural herbal remedy made by an herbalist in Brooklyn to support hot flashes. All of the essentials.

AR *How does your space support your creativity?* RG The way my house supports me is with natural light, so it will elevate my energy when I'm feeling tired, and my room is a cocoon to rejuvenate me so I can go back out into the world and create. All the different spaces in my home support me in living my life.

AR *How do you feel when you're creating?* RG I feel the most authentic and in my natural flow when I'm creating, in any form, whether I'm talking to someone and giving advice, or designing a space.

AR *What life pivots have you had either professionally or emotionally?* RG When I had my children, my business developed around them to prioritize them. As my business grew, so did my children, so it's been very rewarding. Raising my three daughters, with my third being autistic, it made me grow emotionally and professionally in exponential ways. It put everything into order and perspective in my life, and I learned how to prioritize what truly matters. After growing so much emotionally from raising my autistic daughter, I can now handle all the different personalities and potentially stressful situations in business with a calm, logical demeanor, leaving reactive emotions out of it.

AR *How are you living your best life right now?* RG The way I live my best life every day is by being honest and truthful with myself and how I live, versus a fictitious and superficial existence.

PAGE 112
The tortoise shell prominently hung was a gift from Raquel's father to her mother from one of his many trips to Latin America.

RIGHT
The acrylic hand rail, whitewashed floors reminiscent of driftwood, and high-gloss white lacquer shiplap are updates to tradition and reminiscent of Coastal New Southern elements.

BIOGRAPHY
—

CHELSEA ROBINSON INTERIORS
ENTERTAINING TASTEMAKER
INTERIOR DESIGNER

CHELSEA ROBINSON

ALYS BEACH, FLORIDA

This Alys Beach home is a family a retreat defined by classic, understated elegance. An iconic vacation-home community located along the Gulf of Mexico on Florida's panhandle (six miles east of Seaside on Scenic Highway 30A), Alys Beach is a development with a design vision rooted in Bermuda architecture and in the courtyards of Antigua, Guatemala, the colonial capital of Central America. Planned by Duany Plater-Zyberk & Company and Khoury & Vogt Architects, the homes here celebrate a multitude of cultures, which is a trademark of the Coastal New Southern style. For a space like this, Chelsea Robinson instantly saw sisal rugs on the stone floors, raw driftwood, and outdoor planters filled with overdramatized coral. She strives to create juxtaposition in each space, utilizing the contrast between light and dark, modern and old world, and rough and smooth, to create maximum interest and balance. One of Chelsea's design principles is that every room in any house should have at least one antique piece, because antiques immediately ground a space and lend a sense of character and warmth to a palette.

—

AR *Tell us about yourself.* **CR** I was born in Jackson, Mississippi, the perfect Southern small town. I earned my interior design degree at the University of Alabama and minored in art history, spending time abroad in Florence, Italy. I took a master design class under Kelly Hoppen in London, then threw myself into a career that I have loved from day one. Over the past ten years, I have built a successful interior design business and married the love of my life, and have recently been blessed with becoming the mother of two beautiful children. I have clients from all over the country, and I'm blessed to travel to such amazing places to help create beautiful homes. **AR** *What ties you to the South?* **CR** Born and raised—it's in my blood.

OVERLEAF
Chelsea instantly envisioned using natural materials, such as sisal rugs, handcrafted concrete from Peacock Pavers, raw driftwood, and coral to create a fluid indoor-outdoor experience.

AR *What does the Coastal New Southern mean to you and how is this reflected in your home?* **CR** There is something so special about escaping to relax and taking time away from one's everyday routine. My job as a designer is to create an environment that instantly feels like a home away from home, yet a little exotic. That's what being at the beach is like, and I strive to achieve these same feelings in the homes I design and create on the water.

AR *How did you approach the design of your space?* **CR** It is a beach house, so naturally I gravitated toward capturing the beautiful natural surroundings of the Gulf in the home. Since it is a second-home "escape," I wanted the family to feel like they were totally transported from their everyday routine to another world that had an exotic, Mediterranean, fresh vibe, yet was still comfortable enough for them to feel right at home. I also wanted it to be functional for an active family at the beach, so I used indoor/outdoor fabrics on all the upholstery and durable finishes, and made sure I maintained a level of comfort.

AR *Describe your coffee table. What's on it, and why?* **CR** Diptyque candle in Figuier—my favorite home scent—a gorgeous brass candle-holder from Bruges, Belgium, that we picked up in a flea market; an English antique wood tray; a signed copy of Jack Spencer's photography book, which was a gift from a dear client and friend; and the latest McAlpine book, because I adore this design powerhouse. And, of course, fresh flowers.

AR *Living by the water allows a certain sense of calmness. How do you implement that calm in your daily routine?* **CR** By creating time to pause, catch my breath, and enjoy my quiet time and devotionals each day. It seems like life wants you to be busy all the time, but I find myself more productive creatively when I slow down. That is when the magic happens, in the stillness.

"SOMETHING ABOUT THE WATER MAKES YOU STOP AND ENJOY WHAT LIFE IS ALL ABOUT."

BIOGRAPHY

—

COFOUNDER OF OXFORD EXCHANGE
COFOUNDER OF OXFORD DESIGN
COFOUNDER OF OXFORD COMMONS

ALLISON
CASPER ADAMS

TAMPA, FLORIDA

A Tampa native, Allison Casper Adams embodies the concept fueling The Coastal New Southern Style. She loves taking old spaces and breathing new life into them through renovations. As the creator and cofounder of Oxford Exchange, a mixed-use property that consists of creative coworking and event spaces, a bookstore, and several restaurants, she embodies the warmth and connection innate to the old South, coupled with a new way of creating a community through gathering and celebrating shared experiences. And, as a consummate businesswoman and entrepreneur, Allison has also turned Oxford Exchange into a successful brand. As for her own home, she embraces the coast from a worldly perspective and enlisted celebrity designer Nate Berkus to bring her vision to life. With an extensive fine art collection and enviable outdoor space, her home is a livable work of art. The entryway, with a woven table and gold seashells, is at once surf style and sophistication, while her spiral staircase is subtly reminiscent of a ship. The nautical nods continue in the kitchen, which has submarine-like features in the form of metal cabinets and light fixtures. However, what is most striking about the home is the openness. It exudes joy and, like Allison herself, is inspiring in that it always feels like it's coming from a place of "yes."

—

AR *What ties you to the South?* **ACA** I was born and raised in Tampa. I can't imagine living anywhere else.

AR *What inspires you most about the South?* **ACA** The diversity. From Florida to Maryland—different cultures, weather, topography. There are beaches and plantations all in one region.

AR *How do you think creativity unites us across political, social, and economic divides?* **ACA** I think it is easier to find a common ground and connections with the arts. Design, visual arts, and music touch us in ways that are hard to explain but create a feeling we can all understand regardless of our beliefs.

PREVIOUS SPREAD & OVERLEAF
The work of mixed-media artist Brett Murray (page 123) and the large, contemporary etched art by Richard Serra above the sofa (page 128) make a strong visual impact in the space.

AR *How did you approach the design of Oxford Exchange?* **ACA** We wanted to create a place where people could connect and start a conversation. Getting people to unplug and take time to escape was always the goal, so we created spaces where you would feel comfortable and would stay for a while. We wanted to give people the opportunity to linger, and hopefully start a conversation or learn something new.

AR *What is your personal color palette?* **ACA** White, blues, and grays.

AR *What is the key to making a house a home?* **ACA** Collections. Art, objects, photos—whatever has meaning to the owner. More places to sit. I love stools tucked under tables that can double as seats when you are entertaining.

AR *What are your daily rituals?* **ACA** Taking a moment to enjoy where I am. I love our house. We have lived here for eleven years and I am constantly amazed that I like it as much today as the day we moved in.

AR *What is currently on your nightstand?* **ACA** *Daisy Jones & the Six* by Taylor Jenkins Reid, *Strengths Based Leadership* by Tom Rath, and *City of Girls* by Elizabeth Gilbert.

AR *What is your personal mantra?* **ACA** Everything happens for a reason. Sometimes the best ideas have come from trying to find a solution to what we thought were insurmountable problems.

AR *Best life advice you offer, or best life advice you've received?* **ACA** You don't have to be an expert at everything to be successful. You have to believe in yourself and work hard and take risks.

AR *Living by the water allows a certain sense of calmness. How do you implement that calm in your daily routine?* **ACA** There is nothing more beautiful and calming than being on the beach right as the sun sets into the water. I have so many wonderful memories of those moments. And while I do live very close to the water, I don't get to spend as much time there as I would like. However, it doesn't take much for me to be able to take a deep breath and remember that feeling.

"SHARING OUR HOME WITH OTHERS IS HOW WE HONOR IT."

CLEAN EATING IS
THE NEW COCKTAIL HOUR

STYLE

MEYER LEMON
SEA SALT
SHRIMP SALAD

SERVES 4

YOU WILL NEED
—
1½ POUNDS (680 G) SHRIMP, PEELED,
    DEVEINED WITH TAILS LEFT ON
BAMBOO SKEWERS (OPTIONAL)

FOR THE MARINADE:
JUICE OF 1 MEYER LEMON
1 TABLESPOON MEYER LEMON ZEST
2 TABLESPOONS OLIVE OIL
½ TEASPOON SEA SALT
½ TEASPOON GROUND PEPPER
1 TABLESPOON MINCED GARLIC
2 BASIL LEAVES, FINELY CHOPPED

FOR THE DRESSING:
¼ CUP (60 ML) MEYER LEMON JUICE
½ CUP (120 ML) OLIVE OIL
¼ TEASPOON SEA SALT
¼ TEASPOON GROUND PEPPER
1 TEASPOON HONEY
PINCH RED PEPPER FLAKES

FOR THE SALAD:
3 CUPS (60 G) ARUGULA
¼ CUP (25 G) SHAVED PARMESAN
1 AVOCADO, DICED
12 SMALL YELLOW TOMATOES, HALVED
HANDFUL SUGAR SNAP PEAS

Post-beach drinks are a favorite coastal pastime, but the coast can also inspire us to nourish our bodies and taste the freshness of the sea. A big salad is a great way to entertain at sunset. This Meyer Lemon Sea Salt Shrimp Salad packs a bright burst of flavor, and you can offer it alongside refreshing cucumber water or any bubbly of your choice. You can also add any seasonal ingredients that you like. In the summer, I'll grill fresh peaches and corn brushed with this marinade and add them to the salad, along with the shrimp, just before serving. Providing something wholesome is a way to show your guests love and attention in a meaningful way, whether you're on the coast or just in your own backyard.
—
1. Rinse the shrimp with cold water, then place them on ice. 2. Make the marinade: Whisk together the lemon juice, zest, olive oil, sea salt, pepper, garlic, and basil. 3. Add the shrimp to the marinade, then chill in the refrigerator for 30 minutes. 4. Meanwhile, if cooking the shrimp on a grill, soak the bamboo skewers in water and then thread the marinated shrimp onto the soaked skewers. Reserve your extra marinade for use during cooking. 5. Heat the grill or a nonstick grill pan on medium-high heat and cook the shrimp for 2 minutes per side, until the shrimp turn pink and opaque. While cooking, lightly coat the shrimp with the reserved marinade. 6. Make the dressing: Whisk together the lemon juice, olive oil, sea salt, pepper, honey, and red pepper flakes. 7. Make the salad: In a large bowl, combine the arugula, shaved Parmesan, diced avocado, tomatoes, and sugar snap peas, and then toss with the dressing. 8 Add the grilled shrimp on top of the dressed salad, then finish with a little sea salt and fresh pepper. Serve immediately.

CANDID PHOTOS ARE
THE NEW FAMILY PORTRAIT

SUBSTANCE

Beach trips are soaked in memories. Whether it's the idle time, the dog days of summer, or the family togetherness, there is something about being by the coast that takes hold of our minds and begs us to savor the fleeting, precious moments. As a photographer, when I look at my images, I am immediately transported back to all of the senses and emotions felt on a particular day. And with today's technology, we are able to hold on to so much more, by taking videos, or capturing our lives in a photojournalistic way. Instead of recording our memories in posed, smiling photos, we're now taking images and videos of candid scenes in order to more accurately preserve the energy of the moment, and there is no place more photo-worthy than the beach. If you want to make documenting memories interactive and engaging, set out some new/old Polaroid cameras in common spaces along with bowls that fit with your decor, and encourage guests to fill them up with their insta-shots. These moments will provide you with life-giving memories.

COLLECTED

PART 3

Collections not only warm our hearts and remind us that the world is an abundant place, but they also afford us a sense of immortality and posterity. The objects found by those in this category serve as road maps, cementing the weeks, months, and years of a life well-lived. For those who subscribe to the Collected New Southern, objects are imbued with the power of the story behind them—the story of both the object's journey and the collector's search, culminating in the triumphant placement at home. Collectors are a sentimental and soulful tribe with a unique ability to see life in the inanimate, and each of their collections is born from emotion, memory, joy, passion, and a need for growth and expansion. In the pages that follow, you'll see that display methods might vary—stacked, hung, piled, or draped—and objects include everything from vintage watering cans, ceramic pots, and crystals to arrowheads, African art, and flea market finds, but in each home there is a natural movement from room to room. In every space, one fabric plays off another, and around every corner you'll find yet another surprise. There are notes between lovers who are now husband and wife, blueprints hung and framed to represent the hustle of a first-time business owner, and walls covered in black-and-white portraits.

The common thread is blended textures, mixed patterns, mingled surfaces, and clashing colors juxtaposed in the most perfectly imperfect of ways. These homes all have a certain gallery-like opulence of inspiration and liberation, curation and repetition. The collections might be haphazard or orderly, minimal or the-more-the-merrier, but they all started with a creative light and a need to passionately shine it. Many of the homes in the pages ahead are simple canvases for ever-evolving visual story maps created by roadside pickers, online estate-sale scourers, and attendants of grandma's attic. I invite you to sit down, stay awhile, and listen up, because these spaces have tales to tell.

BIOGRAPHY

—

HOST OF HGTV'S *RESTORED BY THE FORDS*

AUTHOR OF *WORK IN PROGRESS*

INTERIOR DESIGNER

PRODUCT DESIGNER

LEANNE FORD

LOS ANGELES, CALIFORNIA

Despite filming her HGTV show *Restored by the Fords*, writing *Work in Progress*, and developing a product line for Target, Leanne Ford still manages to live life as a free spirit, and her home reflects that. Although her space is a California cabin, it's easy to see the influences from her time in Nashville in this Southern love bungalow. With its vertical shiplap, Southern slipcovered couch, and cool barnwood coffee table, the whole space embodies the Collected New Southern. From the layers of white, to a down-to-basics celebration of material, to dried lavender, she has a way of elevating undone and making it look preternaturally beautiful and storied. In this home, the walls do the talking, and they tell a tale of courtship through notes she and her husband have given to each other, concert tickets, plane tickets, and other memories of a life well-loved and well-lived, as well as a love story still unfolding.

—

AR *Tell us about yourself.* LF I am a creative soul, always have been, always will be, no matter what form that creativity takes. I'm in love with my husband, Erik, and we have a little baby girl on the way, who I already feel so soulfully attached to. I have an amazing family. I have been blessed with so much love in my life. Oh, and I love my job!

AR *What ties you to the South?* LF Country music, beautiful Southern souls, and the southern route of a cross-country drive. I also spent years in Nashville, which was heaven.

AR *What does The New Southern mean to you?* LF Design today is a mix of genres, eras, and inspirations. The New Southern pulls from all these inspirations, with a shot of Southern comfort.

AR *How do you see creativity as an important force in today's South, and the country as a whole?* LF When it comes down to it, creativity is the life of a town and of a country.

AR *What does the Collected New Southern mean to you and how is this reflected in your home?* LF I love the style that is coming out of the South right now, eclectic and with a touch of whimsy. I know my time in Nashville influenced my style overall, and I carry that influence with me into all of my projects.

AR *What drew you to your space?* LF It's perfect! It was sold as a teardown in Echo Park, east of Los Angeles, and I couldn't let that happen. I did exactly what everyone warns you against—I got emotionally involved! It was the first house in Echo Park and owned by a silent movie star, Clara Kimball Young, so the history was there, and I wanted to save the little cabin.

AR *How long have you been there?* LF I bought it two years ago and have been working on it since. My husband lives here with me. We were just dating when I bought this place, and he rented a place up the street so we could be close to each other and to the project.

AR *Did you use your surroundings as inspiration?* LF The cabin itself was the entire inspiration. I call it my Little Cabin in the Big City. It's an oasis of trees and woods in the middle of a very big, bustling city.

AR *How did you approach the design of your space?* LF I wanted the design of this cabin to feel original and authentic to the actual 1906 cabin. I wanted the cabin to feel even older than it did when I got my hands on it. Like you walked into a time warp. The decisions we made for the actual structure are all timeless and simple rustic solutions and design elements. Then the furniture brings in all genres, eras, and times. It almost turned into a combination of colonial and space age.

AR *Describe your coffee table. What's on it, and why?* LF I found an old mirrored disco platform that still has marks on it from people dancing! I've loaded it up with books, bowls, trinkets, and my favorite new trick, some pieces of art lying down, almost like they are book covers.

AR *What is your personal color palette?* **LF** Shades of whites and creams, and I always mix in natural elements like wood.

AR *The key to making a house a home?* **LF** Keep any character of the home that you can, or if the house is newer, add some of your own! Texture on the walls and ceiling adds warmth to your space. And always put dimmers on your lights.

AR *What are your rules for displaying collections?* **LF** Keep within a color story. This is the best way for your collections to feel clean and minimal, even if your shelves and home are packed full of treasures! Pick one to three colors to keep your collections in, if you want them to feel cohesive. That way style and vibe can all be mixed but live well together.

AR *How do you decide what to collect?* **LF** Oh, I think it decides for you! Sometimes you are just drawn to things, for no particular reason. But I do love beautiful things that can be useful, such as beautiful bowls and vases.

AR *Top three things you look for when picking at a flea market?* **LF** Mid-century chairs, magical lighting of any style or size, and old concert tees.

AR *What is your general home-design philosophy?* **LF** It's across the board, as it always depends on the home itself. The home tells me what style and aesthetic would live best there. But ease, comfort, and character always seem to be a recurring theme, no matter what style the home takes on.

AR *How does your space support your creativity?* **LF** Our space is filled with our favorite books, art by friends, music—and only things we love. Nothing in this house is here by accident. The whole thing inspires creativity.

RIGHT
This love wall from the time Leanne and her husband first started dating documents all their shared experiences and dreams.

AR *How do you let yourself be vulnerable enough to share your creativity?* **LF** Any creative pursuit is subjective, which means some people will love it, some people will hate it, and that's OK! And I'll tell you what, if no one hates it then no one loves it!

AR *How do you consider yourself a courageous human?* **LF** I am not afraid to fail. Einstein said, "The fear of failure kills creativity." It's so true! You cannot produce new or interesting work without trying things that don't make the cut. It's just part of the process, so be open to failure and you will be open to creativity. That's courage.

AR *What life pivots have you had either professionally or emotionally?* **LF** Life is nothing BUT a plot twist! And failures can be some of the best catalysts taking you where you are supposed to be! Take them as the blessing that they are! And be open to how your life and career are evolving naturally. Don't hold so tight to what you think is "supposed to happen" in your life. I was in fashion for fifteen years before I even considered doing anything in interiors. Our story is never over—be open to the evolution of your life and career and great things can happen!

AR *What is your personal mantra?* **LF** If you aren't making anyone nervous, you aren't doing anything special.

AR *How are you living your best life right now?* **LF** I'm currently being interviewed by you for your book, so that's pretty big! And I am living a life inspired by love, family, and creating every day.

AR *Best life advice you offer, or best life advice you've received?* **LF** "Thy Will Be Done" is my favorite way to live. God has a better plan for us than we could even imagine. So relax and go with the flow; it's all working out just as it should.

"IF YOU AREN'T MAKING ANYONE NERVOUS, YOU AREN'T DOING ANYTHING SPECIAL."

"BE OPEN TO FAILURE AND YOU WILL BE OPEN TO CREATIVITY. THAT'S COURAGE."

BIOGRAPHY

—

AUTHOR OF *SOUL FOOD LOVE*
AUTHOR OF *LUCY NEGRO, REDUX*
HUMAN RIGHTS ACTIVIST
POET
PLAYWRIGHT

CAROLINE RANDALL WILLIAMS

NASHVILLE, TENNESSEE

Caroline Randall Williams grew up in a home steeped in literary tradition. Her mother, Alice, is an author and songwriter, best known for her novel *The Wind Done Gone*, a reinterpretation of *Gone with the Wind*. To this day, Caroline carries on her family's tradition of literary excellence. Recently, the adaptation of her book of poetry, *Lucy Negro, Redux*, published by musician Jack White's Third Man Books, was called "a Nashville miracle" in the *New York Times*. The world knows Caroline as a poet, professor, and food writer, yet she is also a tomato lover, a bourbon drinker, and a sensitive soul with a penchant for jazz. Perhaps it is because of the strength of her lineage that she is unafraid to have a voice and never hesitant to use it, or perhaps it is because she feels so at home in her Southern city. In a place that has become a melting pot, Caroline is a rarity as a Nashville native. Even her home is storied, with Dolly Parton rumored to have once owned it. Though what truly makes her New Southern isn't just her deep ties to the land on which she lives, but the seeds she's planted for future generations who want to grow big there.

—

AR *Tell us about yourself.* CRW I am an artist, a daughter, a friend, an activist, and an educator. I love having people over for dinner more than I love most other things. My dog, Sebastian, is a light of my life, and the strangest creature you'll ever love. Debating someone you respect is, in my opinion, one of the best ways to learn anything.

I grew up here in Nashville, the daughter of a country music songwriter turned novelist—my mother, Alice Randall—and a Nashville-born lawyer. My father's father, Avon Williams Jr., was a civil rights attorney here who got his start during the Woolworth's lunch counter sit-ins of the 1960s. When the building reopened as a restaurant honoring its history, I was excited to be an investor. My great-grandfather was Harlem

Renaissance poet Arna Bontemps. He and my great-grandmother raised my grandmother on the Fisk campus here in Nashville, so I suppose I come by the poem-writing part [of myself] pretty honestly.

AR *What ties you to the South?* CRW The South is in my bones and in my blood. I am of it, and I love it, and I'll always return to it.

AR *What does The New Southern mean to you?* CRW It means looking to the future through the precious frame of what is good and hard about the past.

AR *What inspires you most about the South?* CRW Impossible question. The whole of it is infinitely inspiring.

AR *How do you think creativity unites us across political, social, and economic divides?* CRW If you are making art, if you are living a creative life, then I think your work, necessarily, is to connect with people. Creative work is empathetic. It is an act of witnessing, and truth telling, and lighting dark places. I can't think of anything more universal and uniting.

AR *How do you see creativity as an important force in today's South, and the country as a whole?* CRW We have some hard stories still to tell in this country, and the South is home to some of the most harrowing of the country's hard history. We will need all our art and all of our goodwill to wade through those waters.

AR *What drew you to your space?* CRW Living in my space is a very literal homecoming. This is the house where I was raised. Were that not the case, I would still be drawn to it—its aging grandeur, its airy heights, its wild proportions—but I don't think I could have figured out how to claim it for my own at thirty-one! What a gift to be the second generation to tell the story of a family home. That's what I'm trying to do now. This house is filled with things I picked, things my mother picked, things my parents inherited, picked by my

RIGHT
This vintage Underwood typewriter Caroline and her mother Alice picked from a garage sale serves as a collected bookend.

PAGE 154
Nashville's leading print shop, Hatch Show Print, creates personalized poster invitations for Caroline's family.

"CREATIVE WORK IS EMPATHETIC. IT IS AN
ACT OF WITNESSING, AND TRUTH TELLING,
AND LIGHTING DARK PLACES."

ancestresses. I think that really speaks to how my creative life functions more broadly—much of what I do is informed by or in conversation with the voices and constructions that came before me. It is my privilege to shape art that is a forward-looking heir to those things.

AR *What is your home-design philosophy?* CRW It is, broadly speaking, Southern gothic eclectic streamlined old-school industrial soul. Something like that. There are two-hundred-year-old English chairs, tables made out of found objects and ancient barnwood, solid metal tables, and white denim-covered bucket seats. It's all old and new in here, and dark, and light. Just like the food I cook, the music I love, and the stories I tell when I write.

AR *What is your personal color palette?* CRW I mostly wear black. Or gray. Or brown. Or white. But mostly black. To quote Beyoncé's husband, my philosophy is generally, "all black everything."

AR *What is your favorite room in your house and why?* CRW The kitchen. Because of my grandmother's two-thousand-book cookbook collection, a piano, art done by family and friends, a table made from one of this house's old doors propped up on sawhorses, a teal mini fridge just for sparkling things, every cast-iron vessel you could need, and all of my writing file cabinets. That's why.

AR *Your favorite conversation piece in your home?* CRW The cookbook collection. Especially now that it exists in two places. The kitchen is home to my grandmother's two thousand volumes, and the front hall installation [by Nashville-based Herb Williams] is made up of my godmother Mimi's additional two thousand—give or take—books.

AR *The key to making a house a home?* CRW To me, a house becomes a home when it feels safe, and fresh, and abundant. If I'm afraid to sit on your sofa with a coffee because everything is all white, that's a tough sell on hominess to me. But by the same turn, if I can't find a place to put my coffee cup, that's also a miss. To put it another way: More guests. Less clutter. More home-cooked smells. Less pretense.

AR *How do you consider yourself a courageous human?* CRW I just had the opportunity to be part of a campaign about women who do hard things. In it I was able to voice my truth that being a black body in white spaces is hard. I think that as a woman of color growing up in the South—even a New Southern South—summoning the will to love yourself and rock deeply

in the waters of your own self-worth is an act of courage I undertake every day, as do so many women around me.

AR *How do you let yourself be vulnerable enough to share your creativity?* CRW I generally try not to quote myself in interviews, but I feel like the best answer to this question begins with one of my favorite lines from my book of poetry, *Lucy Negro, Redux*. It says, "Simple and easy ain't the same thing." Being vulnerable enough to share art is not easy. In fact, it feels almost impossible more often than it doesn't. But it is simple. I have no choice but to tell my truth. I have to ring the alarm when I feel it needs ringing. Simple, not easy. I have to keep my eyes open when I learn hard things. Simple, not easy. I have to be an artist because I feel the call from every power anyone believes in, so there is no other real choice. Simple, not easy.

AR *How is the Collected New Southern reflected in the spaces you create?* CRW I think my whole life, my personal ethos, my creative and decorative aesthetic, my inherited and found possessions, and my friendships are a manifestation of the Collected New Southern-ness. If I haven't let that come through by now, then I'm not sure how else to say it.

AR *What life pivots have you had either professionally or emotionally?* CRW I moved to Mississippi in the summer of 2010, two weeks after graduating from college, in order to teach public school in Sunflower County as a Teach for America corps member. Mississippi was, in so many ways, the making of me, the activation of my grown woman's creative voice.

AR *Best life advice you offer, or best life advice you've received?* CRW My mother always says, "success breeds success." She also always reminds me that you don't have to have a Plan B, but that means you have to be creative enough to have infinite approaches to achieving Plan A. Those two pieces of advice go hand in hand for me. I think sometimes we can be myopic about our approach to our dreams; we think we have to proceed in some kind of linear path to reach them. My life and career have altogether disproven that, for me at least. I've learned that if you start something, see it through, and do it well, another door will open. If your heart and your will are in the right place every time, success after success, your Plan A dream will materialize.

AR *How are you living your best life right now?* CRW By making a life in art—what a dream to call that a living.

ALICE RANDALL

author of THE WIND DONE GONE

THE EWING RANDALL WILLIAMS invite you for
BOURBON & BARBECUE
OCTOBER 6th, 2009 8:30PM
2126 BLAIR BOULEVARD RSVP 269-7716

2126 BLAIR BLVD.
MOTOWN
SOUNDS
SOUTHERN
AND SLAVIC
SOUL FOOD
RSVP: 269-7716
FIRST READING FROM & SIGNING OF
THE SECOND NOVEL
6 PM DAVIS·KIDD
PLEASE JOIN US!

THE SERPENT AND THE MOON
SEPTEMBER 25, 2004 · 7 P.M.
2126 BLAIR BLVD.
R.S.V.P. 269-7716

BEE
CHRISTMAS
REAKFAST ON BLAIR
NINE TO NOON
26 BLAIR BLVD

DECEMBER 18, 2011

BIOGRAPHY

—

SEAN ANDERSON DESIGN
ARTIST
INTERIOR DESIGNER

SEAN ANDERSON

MEMPHIS, TENNESSEE

"BEING SURROUNDED BY THINGS THAT TELL MY STORY IS A DAILY REMINDER OF MY PURPOSE AS A CREATIVE."

For Sean Anderson, it's all about process. We live in this world of "likes" and publicity, where everyone is trying to feed an algorithm, but Sean feeds his imagination. With no formal training when it comes to design, Sean instead calls upon raw power and sharp intuition to decide what will make a space look endlessly interesting. With black and dark colors as his basics, he utilizes paint and depth in completely unexpected ways, evidenced by his sultry bedroom. Moody, dripping black candles, a unique gallery wall, and a bow-and-arrow piece gifted by Southern artist Catherine Erb are unique details that complete the collected look in his home. From his assemblage of black-and-white photos of friends and family that populates an entire wall, to an installation that showcases the undersides of beautiful pots and pans, down to his multi-hyphenate job description as an artist and designer, Sean Anderson epitomizes the Collected New Southern—and he gathers more than objects. It's clear he also amasses artist friends, memories, and accumulated skill sets as well.

—

AR *What ties you to the South?* SA My whole life is in the South. I was born here; my family still lives on the same farm I grew up on.

AR *What does The New Southern mean to you?* SA For me, The New Southern is a feeling; it's as simple as that. I don't find it to necessarily be about a particular aesthetic, but rather about the emotion experienced within a space and time.

AR *What inspires you most about the South?* SA The South has a culture unlike anywhere else in the world, much less the country. There is a history here that, for better or worse, has inspired some of the most powerful artistic expressions produced in the twentieth century. The literature, the music, the architecture, the food—there is a common thread that connects these offerings.

AR *How is the Collected New Southern reflected in your home?* SA The Collected New Southern is about telling a story. It's about self-expression, using the things around you as a way of sharing a narrative. The time and energy it takes to procure and curate items for collected spaces is just as much a part of the story as the pieces themselves, which influences how these things are displayed and showcased.

AR *What is your personal color palette?* SA Black and white, all day, every day. I'm also very attracted to juxtaposed earth tones—rich greens, browns, and grays paired with lighter neutral shades and a variety of elemental materials, such as natural fibers, metals, stones, and woods.

AR *The key to making a house a home?* SA Surrounding yourself with things you love, not things you've been programmed to believe to like because they're trendy or readily available. Your home is your space and in turn should be a genuine reflection of you, full of things that tell your story.

AR *What are your rules for displaying collections?* SA I start by reminding myself that there are no rules! I always try to think outside the box and find an original way in which to display them—whether that be in an unusual

pattern or unique framing, or by playing with the scale within a space. There is always a way to take it a step further, and I feel it's important to put your own personal stamp on it.

AR *How do you decide what to collect?* **SA** I don't like to limit myself. I collect anything that I find remotely interesting or objects that I feel will start a conversation. I often choose to collect more obscure pieces that sometimes cause others to stop and question their existence within a space.

AR *Top three things you look for when picking at a flea market?* **SA** Vintage artwork and books, primitive tools—that I often display like pieces of artwork—and eccentric objects that can be used as tabletop accessories in lieu of more traditional ones.

AR *Your favorite online vintage shops?* **SA** 1stdibs and Eneby Home.

AR *Tell us about your mood boards.* **SA** My home is my mood board. I'm most inspired by my environment—if you're surrounded by things that spark creativity, you'll never find yourself short on vision.

AR *How do you think creativity unites us across political, social, and economic divides?* **SA** Creativity is a pure, authentic expression of humanity. Creativity exists everywhere, from the choir lofts of a rural church, to a carpenter's workshop, to the walls of a high street art gallery. Sharing in creative expression is one of the things that will always connect us to one another.

AR *How do you feel when you're creating?* **SA** Alive. Vulnerable. Empowered. Strong. I feel everything I need to in order to push further and be better.

AR *Best life advice you offer, or best life advice you've received?* **SA** "Trust your gut." Once I started listening to this, everything became easier!

LEFT
This bedroom gallery wall contains works by Ashley Finnemore, McKenzie Dove, and Shawn Rivett Designs. The bow-and-arrow piece was gifted by Memphis artist Catherine Erb.

BIOGRAPHY
—
AUTHOR OF *JOY THE BAKER*
CREATOR OF *@DRAKEONCAKE*
YOGA INSTRUCTOR
OWNER OF THE BAKEHOUSE

JOY WILSON

NEW ORLEANS, LOUISIANA

Joy Wilson painted her front door yellow because she wanted to bring more sunshine and happiness into her home. That about sums up her approach to decorating and homemaking. From the lively gallery wall in her dining room to the myriad aprons, mixers, and antique wine-bottle holders she collects, her space is emblematic of the Collected New Southern. Even her online moniker, Joy the Baker, evokes a friendly traditionalism, twinned with a hip online presence that attracts fellow butter-loving devotees. Her home is equally old and new, with the characteristically New Orleanian crocheted throw draped across her chair and homemade biscuits offered as a greeting to guests, alongside bright pops of yellow from fresh lemons in a bowl and a remixed bar cart. However, it is the paper flowers she made (the result of a class she took on how to craft them) sitting on her table that ultimately symbolize the always-growing creative curiosity that fuels her life and her art.

—

AR *Tell us about yourself.* **JW** I'm a baker, writer, teacher, and all-around curious person. My refrigerator is filled with butter and I love life, every bit.

AR *What ties you to the South?* **JW** My grandmother moved from Alabama to California years and years ago, so part of my soul is rooted in the South.

AR *What does The New Southern mean to you?* **JW** Southern culture is such an indelible and unique part of American culture. The New Southern feels like a modern take on its beauty and pace of life.

AR *What inspires you most about the South?* **JW** There's something almost indescribable in the air down South, especially in New Orleans. It's a thickness, and spirit you can open your arms and hold on to. I'm so inspired by the color, culture, music, and pace of life down South.

LEFT
The kitchen is an important place for Joy, and elements throughout the space demonstrate this centrality. Baking utensils used as styling accessories are layered throughout the home.

AR *How do you think creativity unites us across political, social, and economic divides?* **JW** The ability to express yourself is universal. That invitation is open to all here in New Orleans.

AR *How do you see creativity as an important force in today's South, and the country as a whole?* **JW** In New Orleans it's as though everyone is an artist of some sort. Creativity is steeped into the bones of this city. Creation is essential to this city and an encouraged expression. There is no wrong expression here and it feels really liberating.

AR *What drew you to your space?* **JW** I've lived in my house in the Bywater for three years now. I was drawn to it because the kitchen is the center of the house. I cook and gather people every week, so being able to be in the kitchen and be part of the gathering was essential to me. The light felt calming, and I knew it could be a space that I could fill with new friends, food, and laughter. I also have filled the space with antiques from northern Louisiana, salvaged wood shelves from the French Quarter, pieces I've collected from estate sales, and pops of color for a vibrant feel.

AR *What is your favorite room in your house and why?* **JW** My favorite room in the house is the main room—the front door leads into a big dining room, open kitchen, bar, and sitting area. I'm always in the kitchen whipping something up, and when I entertain, everyone ends up in the kitchen. I love that the main room in my house is really just a huge kitchen. So when people gather and cluster around a cheese plate I'm making, there's plenty of room for everyone!

AR *What does the Collected New Southern mean to you and how is this reflected in your home?* **JW** A collection of personal tokens makes a house a home. For me, these are a lot of kitchen tokens and art I've found in the South

"MY REFRIGERATOR IS FILLED WITH BUTTER AND I LOVE LIFE, EVERY BIT."

and on all the roads that have led me south. They fill this New Orleans house with memories and warmth.

AR *How do you decide what to collect?* JW I'll collect anything passed down from my grandmothers and anything that supports those tokens.

AR *Top three things you look for when picking at a flea market?* JW I'm always looking for unique silver serving pieces, small plates with old patterns, and vintage glassware.

AR *Your favorite online vintage shops?* JW There are so many hidden gems on Etsy, but I still think the best vintage shopping is an elusive, small-town, stars-align discovery.

AR *What are your daily rituals?* JW I practice yoga in my space every day—I set aside at least a few moments to light a candle, breathe, and move a bit. I also spend every morning in my kitchen, slowly making myself coffee, listening to records, reading the news, and settling into the day.

AR *How does your space support your creativity?* JW This space is the hub of my creativity. I create, test, and photograph recipes in this space—always making a huge mess in the kitchen. Most importantly, every weekend I welcome a dozen people into the space and teach baking workshops. My hope is that we all share in the creativity that this space calls up.

AR *How do you feel when you're creating?* JW Every day is different, but the good days feel like a steady flow of endless ideas big and small. There are plenty of rough days that feel like walking through knee-high water, but I take the trudge with the good.

AR *What does creativity mean to you?* JW Creativity is the expression of self, in all the ways that the self manifests—in the things that I make with my hands, the words I write, the songs I sing badly in my car, the physical space I create for myself, the way I make my friends feel. It's everything!

AR *How do you let yourself be vulnerable enough to share your creativity?* JW Vulnerability feels like an essential part of creativity to me. I think of it as an offering and a service to one another—the thing that makes us feel human and more connected to one another.

AR *What is your personal mantra?* JW I have two: You're not the kind of girl who settles; keep not settling. And when I'm working my mantra is simple: Keep doing things. I especially have to repeat this one when there's a giant pile of dishes in the sink.

AR *Best life advice you offer, or best life advice you've received?* JW Say yes even if, and especially if, you're scared.

AR *How do you consider yourself a courageous human?* JW I believe in myself and I'm willing to take chances.

AR *How are you living your best life right now?* JW I stop to sit on the porch with friends and wine. That's living my best life.

ABOVE & RIGHT
A collection of personal tokens makes a house a home, from the paper flowers Joy crafts as a hobby to the vintage French wine racks in the living room.

OVERLEAF
A portrait of Joy's aunt adorned with a colorful Etsy-style garland is centered on her gallery wall in the dining room of this 1900s shotgun home.

BIOGRAPHY

—

SINGER-SONGWRITER

OWNER OF WHITE'S MERCANTILE

OWNER OF WHITE'S ROOM AND BOARD

OWNER OF H. AUDREY BOUTIQUE

HOLLY WILLIAMS

NASHVILLE, TENNESSEE

Holly Williams is a jill-of-all-trades. A mother, a shop owner with several thriving locations, a musician who sings at the Grand Ole Opry, and an Airbnb host, Holly generalizes in everything entrepreneurial and specializes in being a badass. This space is one of her Airbnbs, and also the place that she called home before the renovations took place. In the presence of collections, we automatically connect with the humanity of intentionally bringing gathered objects back to a treasured and personal home. To choose this form of decor for a temporary space is an act of genius, acknowledging those who come to stay are seeking the experience of home rather than hotel. Holly is able to evoke that experience of rootedness, erasing any traces of transience, while creating a space full of color and warmth that guests can imagine, if only for a few days, is their very own.

—

AR *Tell us about yourself.* HW I love music, storytelling, and songwriting with a deep, deep passion. Retail, renovation, business, design, all of that is awesome! I believe we can change the world with our words.

AR *What ties you to the South?* HW My roots! Mama and her family hail from Louisiana, and Daddy is from Alabama.

AR *What does The New Southern mean to you?* HW Innovation and progress while sticking to our core values of kindness and welcoming. Our food has expanded, we have chic boutique hotels, our interiors can compete with any metropolitan city—ours just have that extra dose of warmth, usually with granny's oil paintings and some heirloom blankets on display.

AR *How do you see creativity as an important force in today's South, and the country as a whole?* HW Our chefs are taking "Southern food" to another level—Tandy Wilson of City House, Sean Brock of Husk—while our artists, like Chris Coleman, our photographers; and our designers are getting calls from across the country. I think people are recognizing the crazy talent pool that lives here and can create things far outside the box, but who remain some of

the loveliest people to work with that you will ever come across.

AR *What drew you to your space?* HW This was a tiny Victorian cottage from 1892 that I've been madly in love with ever since I first laid eyes on it fifteen years ago, and used to rent it. Now I've turned it into a luxury nightly rental experience, and I haven't even slept here since the renovation! My surroundings have to be inspiring to keep my creative brain going. Inspiring doesn't mean expensive. I splurge on things like a great bathtub, kitchen counters, lighting, and wallpaper—things that will stand the test of time. But it's incredible what $150 can get you at an antique mall. The kitchen walls are lined with cheap old plates I found at local antique shops, along with the old photographs and chest of drawers. I love to be surrounded by stories, and wonder who lived here, played here, used this wooden rolling pin before me! I try to honor history by curating old stuff, and I think it's important that we live our lives honoring the past, talking to our elders and decorating by reusing things with a story. That's my favorite way to live, to explain to our children how much something in our home means to us.

AR *Describe your signature aesthetic in three words.* HW Nostalgic, modern, feminine.

AR *What are your rules for displaying collections?* HW Plates piled together, gold frames hanging in an unplanned wall display—I like the quirky moments.

AR *How do you decide what to collect?* HW I've always been drawn to old ironstone, pewter plates, gold gilt frames, and paintings.

AR *What is your personal color palette?* HW I have a mad passion for hints of blush, deep reds, bold but cool blues, and, of course, white and black layered up with antiques.

AR *The key to making a house a home?* HW A home needs more items that mean something to you, that have a story behind them. Less kitchen gadgets you haven't used in five years and more of grandma's recipe cards. Items that feel like they will stay with you through your life and possible moves.

LEFT
Immediately greeting you when you walk into the fresh pink door of this 1890s cottage are flea market finds and Cole & Son's soft clouds wallpapered overhead.

"I TRY REALLY HARD TO BE LIVING IN THE PRESENT MOMENT WITH WHATEVER I'M DOING."

AR *What does creativity mean to you?*
HW For some reason, God made me an open book, which makes many family members uncomfortable when I'm writing for a new album! I meet people on airplanes and they know my life story within three minutes. I think if we realize how short we are here for, and that God has given us a specific time on this earth, and we remember that in one hundred years the hurtful words or opinions of others won't matter, then it helps us follow our dreams with vulnerability, to show the world something that deeply matters to us.

AR *How are you living your best life right now?* **HW** I try really hard to be living in the present moment with whatever I'm doing. Whether this is baking cookies with the girls, working in the office, performing a concert, working on a house renovation, or opening new stores as I'm growing the White's Mercantile brand, I try to be fully present. Bob Dylan once said, "He not busy being born is busy dying," and it's something to live by. I don't take that to mean that we should stay busy all the time, but I do try to keep learning like a child, and I work on being born in every aspect of my passions. And "being born" can mean taking a nap with your toddler when you need rest and recovery.

AR *How do you consider yourself a courageous human?* **HW** I have a major risk tolerance, which pretty much terrifies everyone around me! I have taken some major business risks, starting with my first clothing boutique in 2007. On the music side, my first creative risk was driving my mom's Suburban around the country with a guitar, playing wherever I could. I wanted to create in many forms—songwriting, retail, design. My philosophy is: "When in doubt, figure it out." I usually say yes to things, trusting my gut that I will work hard to figure out the next steps even if I don't know 100 percent what the heck I am doing! I'm either crazy or courageous, I suppose. I try to be a courageous mama and allow my babies to see hard work, and lots of love.

AR *Best life advice you offer, or best life advice you've received?* **HW** There's the old saying, "Things turn out best for the people that make the best out of the way things turn out." I've always loved that. The key to life is acceptance, not expectation of how it should be. That took me a long time to learn, and to finally grasp and take hold of. It's not what happens to us in life; it's how we react to it. It's not getting angry with God; it's trusting he will guide you through the storm no matter how hard the wind blows.

BIOGRAPHY

—

AUTHOR OF *NUTRITION STRIPPED*
WELLNESS COACH
REGISTERED DIETITIAN NUTRITIONIST

MCKEL KOOIENGA

NASHVILLE, TENNESSEE

RIGHT
McKel sprinkles collected
crystals around the house.
They are not only symbolic
of purity and cleansing
energy, but also serve as
soulful styling elements.

Living a collected life is about more than gathering like objects together; there is also the concept of being collected in a human sense. Having lived many lives, McKel Kooienga has been shaped by the collection of her past experiences, which have formed the different facets of her personality. Mindful, grounded, and self-aware, McKel reflects these traits in her home through her meditation floor pillow, layered art above the sofa, and her grouping of plants, which signals her earthiness. A leader in the health and wellness space, McKel developed a way for anyone to access nutrition education, using digital resources to disseminate her teachings. Her home is her incubator, a place where she lives, creates, cooks, and nourishes, always amassing new experiences to add to her continuously collected life.

—

AR *Tell us about yourself.* MK I'm here to help others take care of themselves through nourishing their mind, body, and spirit. I use nutrition as the vehicle for self care. I also work with people on habit change through learning—and applying—daily practices that, in turn, make long-term change.

AR *What ties you to the South?* MK Community. Nature. Opportunity. It feels like home and has been mine for many years.

AR *What does The New Southern mean to you?* MK Thinking outside the box, owning your unique creativity, and pushing the boundaries of tradition.

AR *What inspires you most about the South?* MK Genuine Southern hospitality—it's unlike any part of the US I've visited, with this infectious charm, kindness, and community-driven mindset.

AR *How is the Collected New Southern reflected in your home?* MK For me, collected means a layered approach to self-care. For example, a collection of items that make me feel nourished, such as pantry items; ones that make me feel grounded and centered, such as a journal, sage, crystals, or a plant; and ones that make me feel a sense of ritual and routine, such as a tea set with loose-leaf nettle and honey.

AR *How did you approach the design of your space?* MK My husband and I wanted our first home to be a space where we could take the time to experiment with our design aesthetic and taste, with future goals of building our dream home surrounded by nature. We are also at a chapter in our lives where we both want to be closer to downtown Nashville for our company.

AR *What is your favorite room in your house and why?* MK In our loft, my favorite room is the kitchen! We spend so much time in here for work but also quality time cooking together. It's the heart of our home.

AR *Describe your coffee table. What's on it, and why?* MK There is a large, beautiful clay bowl with an endless number of sage bundles. I burn sage daily as part of a morning meditation ritual and it's very special to me. The components include a brass singing bowl, crystals, candles, and a few books for visual inspiration.

AR *Tell us about your mood boards.* MK Most of my vision boards relate to feelings, vibes, or visions I want to manifest from nature, people interactions, color palettes, or patterns I'm drawn to.

AR *How do you see creativity as an important force in today's South, and the country as a whole?* MK The more people step into their own power and self-worth, the more their creativity flows, and that can cause waves of change

AR *How does your space support your creativity?* MK We have a lot of plants in our home, and I'm endlessly inspired by nature.

AR *What does creativity mean to you?* MK Expressing yourself freely and without judgment or confinement.

**"I SHOW UP FOR MYSELF FULLY SO I
CAN SHOW UP FOR OTHERS."**

"THE KEY TO LIFE IS
ACCEPTANCE, NOT EXPECTATION
OF HOW IT SHOULD BE."

RIGHT
This living space is
accented with wall art
by Benjy Russell and
beautiful Anthropologie
home furniture elements,
including a fringed floor
meditation pillow.

AR *How do you let yourself be vulnerable enough to share your creativity?* **MK** I think it goes back to having a high sense of self-worth and knowing that I can only be one way in this universe, and that's showing up fully—meaning being confident and connected with who I am to let creativity flow and be free.

AR *How do you consider yourself a courageous human?* **MK** Owning a company has challenged me to be brave and courageous. It takes tremendous amounts of self-confidence, emotional resilience, and keeping the momentum of progressing toward my North Star of helping others. With all the obstacles I come across, the rewards I reap from those challenges taste that much sweeter.

AR *What are your daily rituals?* **MK** Cooking, meditation, and self-care reflection time are part of my daily rituals, and having a space conducive to those things is so important!

AR *What is currently on your nightstand?* **MK** A sea-salt lamp, a photo of my husband and me, and a lavender pillow spray.

AR *How are you living your best life right now?* **MK** Checking in with myself daily and practicing gratitude for all that I have and all that I am in this very moment. It also helps to wake up each day knowing that I'm putting my feet forward to help others!

AR *Best life advice you offer, or best life advice you've received?* **MK** Remember not to take yourself or life so seriously.

DIGITAL VINTAGE STORES ARE THE NEW FLEA MARKET

STYLE

There is something comforting about walking into a flea market and feeling the stories of the items around you, but there are now two types of "picker" experiences. Those who collect can still get the thrill of discovery at a local market or antique store, taking the time to hunt through brick-and-mortar merchandise, but they can also search for specific items from dealers across the country from the convenience of home, among a proliferation of websites selling one-of-a-kind wares. The categories and descriptions online can also be great teaching tools to understand styles from contemporary, to traditional, to mid-century modern, to vintage French Louis XVI. The online experience adds a whole new dimension to antique shopping and allows anyone with an internet connection to create a varied space full of texture, character, and layers.

Here are some of my favorite online haunts. Happy hunting.

—

CHAIRISH This fantastic vintage decor resource out of San Francisco was founded by Anna Brockway and her husband. It offers one-of-a-kind pieces, atypical finds, and art. I love this site for side tables, chairs, and bowls. The site also has a detailed search engine and educational resources to understand the pieces and their history.

ONE KINGS LANE This is one of the most beautiful and editorial sites. They also have a helpful blog. This is the perfect place to shop for old and new. Their endless inventory makes it so that you can find anything you're looking for, as well as inspiration for miles.

ETSY This site is my number one secret (though not anymore) for vintage Oushaks, hemp kilims, Beni Ourain rugs, and Lithuanian linen throws. It is also a useful tool for anyone who doesn't have an interior designer, because you can customize items like pillows and befriend dealers and shop owners, making your own home-goods contacts.

JAYSON HOME The global site of the Chicago-based landmark store has a curated, select offering. I always peruse the sale side of their vintage finds, where they offer great deals. It's a finely edited selection, for those who are easily overwhelmed by too much choice.

COLLECTED IS THE NEW TCHOTCHKE

SUBSTANCE

The collectors featured in this book are intentional, mindful, and methodical about their collections. Their pieces add character and storytelling to their spaces and are born from soulful choices that speak to the collector on a deep level. Instead of rummaging yard sales for deals and disparate pieces, they look for items that make their hearts sing. The key is tight curation and categorization by shape, genre, or color. While sometimes you don't know exactly what you want to collect, pay attention to what you gravitate toward. It will quickly become clear what you're drawn to and then you can plan for display. You can also base your collection on the things you care about most, whether you're a photographer with a vintage camera collection, a musician collecting antique instruments, or you're making your home a space open for entertaining by collecting pre-Civil War bowls, cutting boards, or chairs. Collecting is also an affordable and beautiful way to begin an art collection.

PREPPY

PART 4

In this chapter, we're tossing out the rules of exclusivity and throwing the doors open to freedom of expression and pattern play at its best. The Preppy New Southern style is exemplified by casual Americana blended with wild and worldly graphic elements at play, like stripes, buffalo checks, and color combined in unexpected ways. In the pages that follow, you'll find gutsy entrepreneurs, fearless designers, and bold artists, and in their spaces you'll see endearing touches of whimsy mixed in among the personalized paper goods and blue-and-white ginger jars. Big on Southern entertaining, the Preppy New Southerners are partial to large rooms meant for gathering and pops of tangerine color to bring spaces to life. Their fashion is intertwined with their design choices, favoring floral patterns, gingham, and denim for both furniture and weekend wear.

The Preppy New Southern flag waves proudly, crafted out of seersucker and Cape Cod plaid. With an ode to deconstructed formality, traditional blues and soft pink accents fill spaces, accentuated by quirk and humor. Don't be fooled by their sweet Southern drawls, these women are forward-thinking bosses, proudly taking up space in the world. So, slide on those loafers and let's head out to the backyard to stroll among the boxwood, admire the peonies and poppies, and dream up big, big plans for the future.

BIOGRAPHY

—

CAITLIN WILSON DESIGN
TEXTILE AND PRODUCT DESIGNER
INTERIOR DESIGNER

CAITLIN WILSON

DALLAS, TEXAS

"I AM UNAPOLOGETICALLY MYSELF AND GUTSY TO THE CORE."

Standing in front of one of her own striking floral patterns in a gingham dress fitting for both her home and brand, Caitlin Wilson literally embodies the style that put her on the map. A San Francisco native who was originally an interior designer, Caitlin has since branched out and created her own dynamic lifestyle brand, with textiles, rugs, furniture, lighting, and more. In her former Portland, Oregon, home, Caitlin brought a quintessential New Southern feel to the Pacific Northwest (she has since moved to Dallas, Texas, and opened two showrooms in Dallas and Houston). Caitlin has always described herself as "preppy to the core," but having lived abroad and on both the East and West Coasts, she is now a mélange of all the "prep" she's seen. Her take on the Preppy New Southern is rooted in traditional design and classic novelties like monograms, ginger jars, and layers of collectibles such as gold frames and vintage books from her travels. While her navy-blue-and-white buffalo check chairs and pink accents make a bold statement, her dining room is also a reminder that family dinners and gatherings are always at the center of how this husband-and-wife team operates. With four children, it's this putting-family-first motto, and not necessarily the cowhide rug or denim sofa, that makes their communal living spaces so darn warm and inviting.

—

AR *Tell us about yourself.* CW My husband and I had the unique opportunity to live and work overseas right after we had our first child. We moved to London, Dubai, and Hong Kong for two years and it was incredibly enriching.

I launched my business out of the third bedroom of our Philadelphia apartment when my husband was in business school and I was pregnant with my second child. My travels and my textile line are a huge part of my story. I am so grateful for the opportunities and feel blessed by every place and person I've met along the way.

AR *What ties you to the South?* CW I moved to Tennessee from California when I was eleven and spent five formative years there— years that I didn't realize would influence my taste and impact my style so much later in my life.

AR *What inspires you most about the South?* CW The South is such a unique, charming place. I love the character of the buildings, the traditional architecture, the love of color and pattern, and the warm hospitality of the people. I especially love that people know how to slow down and enjoy life.

AR *What does it mean to be a creative individual in the South?* CW We're a part of a new movement of movers and shakers in a place that is thriving and taking off in the creative fields. From interiors to product design, photography, and fashion, there is a lot of buzz in the South.

AR *How do you think creativity unites us across political, social, and economic divides?* CW Creativity is a universal language that everyone engages in and utilizes to some extent. Design is a part of our everyday life and I'm grateful we live in a day and era where creativity is truly celebrated.

AR *How did you approach the design of your space?* CW I wanted our home to be a blend of a few places I'd been and homes I'd loved. I wanted a traditional colonial feel with a formal living room with paneling, but I wanted the rest of the home to feel casual and comfortable with shiplap and natural woods.

AR *What is your personal color palette?* **CW** Blues in every shade—soft blue, bright French blue, navy blue. . . and always a touch of pink!

AR *What is your favorite room in your house and why?* **CW** My home office is the first room you see and it just feels interesting and bold. I love how it tells our story through art and collections we've curated over the years.

AR *The key to making a house a home?* **CW** Collections, family photos, meaningful art, and layers. I think homes need less decor on the walls and more dimension through interesting furniture arrangements.

AR *Essential ingredients to produce the perfect garden party?* **CW** My personal garden party would include French music, sparkling lemonade, and baskets full of chocolate chip cookies!

AR *How does your space support your creativity?* **CW** Light is especially important for me to feel happy and creative, and the music room covered in wallpaper and flooded with light feels heavenly while I sit and work.

AR *What does creativity mean to you?* **CW** Creativity is a place for me—a mental state of mind when ideas are flowing freely. It's where I feel the most alive and where I truly feel like I'm utilizing my gifts.

AR *How do you consider yourself a courageous human?* **CW** I took a leap of faith nearly eight years ago and have been sharing myself and my work pretty boldly since then. I have been working without much fear for so long now that it's just a part of who I am.

AR *What life pivots have you had either professionally or emotionally?* **CW** I have to pivot every time I have a baby, because it's physically impossible for me to be at the office as much as I'm needed. I'm always learning to delegate and trust my team, and even though it requires me to lose a bit of control, it allows me to use my time on what I'm best at and most needed for.

AR *What is your personal mantra?* **CW** Make it happen. I've always been a driven person. From the time I was a little girl, I've been driven to do things that others hadn't done. If I wanted to do something or to learn a skill or talent, I'd just go for it. I'm unapologetically myself and gutsy to the core.

AR *Best life advice you offer, or best life advice you've received?* **CW** I always try to remember that everyone has been given gifts and we all have something unique we can share. No one person's perspective will be the same as another's, so we can and should appreciate each other's talents without judgment or envy.

RIGHT
Combining French blue, navy, and seafoam green artisanal vases with a classic blue-and-white patterned bowl creates a picture-perfect Preppy New Southern moment.

BELOW
Caitlin is known for the casual and chic Buffalo Check products she designs and sells. The soft-blue and pink color scheme woven throughout the home sets the stage for deconstructed formalities.

"I ALWAYS TRY TO
REMEMBER THAT EVERYONE
HAS BEEN GIVEN GIFTS AND WE
ALL HAVE SOMETHING
UNIQUE WE CAN SHARE."

BIOGRAPHY
—
FOUNDER OF PENCIL & PAPER CO.
LIFESTYLE TASTEMAKER
INTERIOR DESIGNER

GEN
SOHR

NASHVILLE, TENNESSEE

Gen Sohr and her husband, Benjamin, are proof that opposites attract. While Ben favors clean, modern, and spare, taking cues from his architecture background, Gen is drawn to preppy vintage finds, color, pattern, and layers. Yet it is the combination of their two styles that forms the design magic behind their brand. Before launching Pencil & Paper Co., the duo had been designing homes for some time, but it was the publicity surrounding their home in the 12 South area of Nashville that catapulted their brand. Their design projects are filled with saturated interiors and high doses of white that hark back to the bright whites and piles of sunshine that filled Gen's home growing up in Miami. An innate problem solver, she sees each room as a puzzle, the pieces of which can be placed perfectly together to garner the best result. While Gen sees creative control as one of the best things about owning her own business, the true freedom is having the flexibility to be available as a mother for her son during the day, then continue to work feverishly into the night puzzling over a project that excites her. Like most entrepreneurs, she works more now, but she knows it's a small price to pay for living life on her own terms.

—

AR *Tell us about yourself.* **GS** I'm persistent, creative, and a design lover.

AR *What ties you to the South?* **GS** Family.

AR *What does The New Southern mean to you?* **GS** Embracing traditions—both old and new.

AR *What inspires you most about the South?* **GS** When I moved to Nashville, I was instantly in love. I loved the tradition, the Southern hospitality, the manners. I'd lived in all of these big cities for most of my life and

Nashville was this breath of fresh air. I instantly felt safe, and there was something lovely about letting my guard down, because there was an incredible warmth coming from the people that I'd never before experienced. When we first moved here, Ben said, "You don't have to lock the doors. Don't worry about it—it's Nashville."

AR *How do you see creativity as an important force in today's South, and the country as a whole?* **GS** We moved back to Nashville—Benjamin's hometown—in 2003, from San Francisco, to be near family, but also to be able to have a creative impact in a less crowded playing field. To be a part of the creative growth of Nashville and the South has been a true joy.

AR *How do you think creativity unites us across political, social, and economic divides?* **GS** I embraced Instagram because it reminded me of the magazine editorial world, and I love fashion, interiors, taking photos, and every aspect of how that comes together like in a magazine layout. One of the most valuable things about social media, though, is its ability to connect people. Finding a community of people online that shares your love of style, design, and travel allows you to connect to so many people with whom you might not otherwise cross paths.

AR *How does your space support your creativity?* **GS** Being in space that is light-filled, with color, patterns, and art, gives me joy daily.

AR *What is your favorite room in your house and why?* **GS** I love our sunroom for the warm sunlight and nostalgic feel. The original homeowner built it for his mom to have her girlfriends over. It has the most charming original marble mosaic floors. We pretty much left it as we found it—just brightened it up with a fresh coat of white paint, which solves all problems!

RIGHT
Pencil & Paper Co. created this saturated Alphabet Art, which provides a fun and approachable way to style around bright, Preppy New Southern hues.

"PASSION, HAPPINESS, AND ENTHUSIASM ARE THE GREATEST PREDICTORS OF SUCCESS."

LEFT
Parisian-inspired bistro chairs from Ballard Designs complement the Regina Andrew lighting and La Cornue range.

AR *Describe your signature aesthetic in three words.* **GS** Happy, colorful, eclectic. The wallpaper pattern in the powder room sums up my aesthetic. It's based on a traditional and vintage print while incorporating a modern feel with its graphics and use of color.

AR *What is your personal color palette?* **GS** Orangey red, blue, and white.

AR *How do you consider yourself a courageous human?* **GS** I'm a quick and decisive decision maker and usually don't second guess myself.

AR *What is currently on your nightstand?* **GS** A collection of vintage dishes and boxes to hold bits and bobs, layered art, magazines, and fresh flowers.

AR *What life pivots have you had either professionally or emotionally?* **GS** Leaving the safety of working for a big company with a coveted title to start over and create Pencil & Paper Co. with my husband.

AR *What is your personal mantra?* **GS** Color makes me happy.

AR *What does the Preppy New Southern mean to you and how is this reflected in your home?* **GS** Colorful, pattern-filled, mixed with heritage and tradition.

AR *Essential ingredients to produce the perfect garden party?* **GS** Sunshine, tons of potted plants, pretty patterned linens, rattan, fresh flowers, and inspiring conversations!

AR *How are you living your best life right now?* **GS** I helped others create world-renowned brands for many years (Old Navy, Victoria's Secret, the Body Shop). The last six years of building our own brand has been so creatively fulfilling. Running our own business allows us the freedom to travel and make our own schedule. I'm beyond grateful each day to be able to pick up my son from school and truly take in this time. I only wish I could go back in time and tell my younger self to leave the safety of corporate America much, much sooner.

BIOGRAPHY

—

FOUNDED BY REESE WITHERSPOON
LIFESTYLE AND CLOTHING BRAND

DRAPER JAMES

NASHVILLE, TENNESSEE

@DRAPERJAMES

greetings
from...
DRAPER
JAMES
Nashville, Tennessee

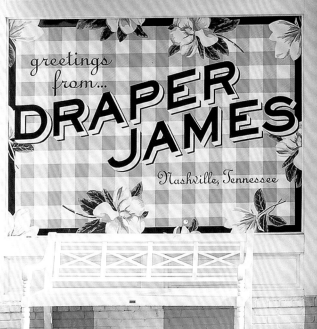

LEFT
The Draper James
brand communicates
confidence, femininity,
and a courageous Southern
spirit through the interior
design of its stores and its
merchandise created by
Reese Witherspoon and
head clothing designer
Kathryn Sukey.

Draper James founder Reese Witherspoon grew up in a traditional Southern family and wanted to create a brand that spoke to the time-honored sense of hospitality with which she was raised, while integrating a modern playfulness and whimsy. With pieces such as its signature fabric bags adorned with Southernisms like "y'all" and trinkets bearing the words "pretty as a peach" and "call your mama," the brand speaks to women like a spirited, close Southern friend would. The store is also filled with books, a nod to Reese's wildly popular book club, and in fact feels like a club itself—it has a look so unique that each location feels like part of the same big Draper James world. With the iconic stripes for which designer Mark D. Sikes is known, and liberal use of the brand's signature preppy blue, the space conjures thoughts of sweet tea and front porches. It comes as no surprise that the Draper James stores have become tourist destinations, while the online site offers women all over the country a piece of Southern style.

—

AR *Where does Draper James call home?*
DJ Draper James was founded in Nashville, Tennessee, but we also have locations in Lexington, Kentucky; Dallas, Texas; and Atlanta, Georgia.

AR *Tell us about Draper James in a few sentences.* DJ Draper James was created by Reese Witherspoon because she wanted to take everything she loves about the South—the grace, charm, and style—and bring it into people's homes, no matter where they live. As the brand has grown and evolved, every product and story we tell continues to be steeped in Southern charm, designed for real life, and unapologetically pretty.

AR *What ties Draper James to the South?* DJ Reese Witherspoon founded Draper James as a way to honor her Southern heritage, and in particular her grandparents, who were, and still are, the greatest influences in her life: her grandmother, Dorothea Draper, and her grandfather, William James Witherspoon.

AR *What does The New Southern mean to Draper James?* DJ Reese started Draper James because she noticed a boom of cultural growth in the South and simultaneously felt a void in what both fashion and lifestyle brands were offering the world. As a brand, we celebrate the spirit of the South today and continue to share the authentic stories and messages for which the region is known.

AR *What inspires Draper James most about the South?* DJ The people, the food, the parties, the places. The grace and charm of the South is something we try to re-create every single day.

AR *How does Draper James think creativity unites us across political, social, and economic divides?* DJ As a brand, we stand for inclusivity and kindness, which are two ideas we consider when designing our pieces.

AR *Describe Draper James's signature aesthetic in three words.* DJ Fun, pretty, versatile.

AR *How did Draper James approach the design of the store?* DJ Reese wants the store to feel like "the modern Southern woman's home." Interior designer Mark D. Sikes, who decorated the shop and also worked on Reese's own home in Nashville, gave the space an abundance of domestic and traditional touches: The cash wrap resembles a kitchen island with a marble counter top, complete with stools around the perimeter; several cozy and intimate seating areas beckon you to stay awhile; and the back entrance has the look and feel of a mudroom, with a bench to sit on and hooks for stashing coats.

AR *What is Draper James's personal color palette?* DJ Draper James Blue. The color can be found on everything from our logo, to handbags and dresses, to the photogenic blue-and-white striped wall outside our Nashville and Atlanta stores.

AR *What are Draper James's favorite ways to pattern play?* DJ Life, and your wardrobe, should be fun! Every Draper James collection includes some sort of pattern—whether it's a plaid, a floral, or a fun print you've never seen anywhere else. Our in-house design team creates these patterns, often using aspects of the South as inspiration, and it's so exciting to see them come to life.

"LIFE, AND YOUR WARDROBE,
SHOULD BE FUN!"

BIOGRAPHY

—

HAYLEY MITCHELL ART
COLOR CONNOISSEUR

HAYLEY MITCHELL

AUSTIN, TEXAS

RIGHT
Hayley's stairwell is filled
with whimsical pattern play
and pops of pinks and blues
as she adorns the walls with
her children's artwork.

Hayley Mitchell is a woman juggling entrepreneurship and life. She reminds us that we can have it all, just not all on the same day. She is approachable and as saturated with wit and personality as the pops of pinks and blues in the cubist faces she creates. Her art is emblematic of the facelift the Preppy New Southern is giving to traditional Southern sensibilities with the messages of inclusiveness and honesty, while the striped runner, slipcovered sofas, and blue-and-white accents in her home speak to an old Southern charm. Sold by One Kings Lane and countless other outlets, Hayley's art often seems composed of simple geometric shapes, but it evokes strong and powerful feminine "goddess-like" energy that epitomizes The New Southern woman.

—

AR *Tell us about yourself.* **HM** I am an artist and mother of four living in Austin, Texas, with my husband, Ben. My grandmother, also an artist, would teach me, give me free rein of her studio, and take me to museums. She pushed me to take risks and make mistakes, and encouraged me to not be so technically perfect. When I was nine, she took me to Paris for the first time. I credit that early immersion with laying the foundation of my artistic path. Much of my work centers around women and, in short, is a celebration of the female form and the power women possess. A lot of my work is inspired by my unexpected journey into motherhood, and the realization that everyone is someone's child. It opened my eyes to the struggles and triumphs of the women that came before me and the hardworking women around me.

AR *What ties you to the South?* **HM** I am a Texan through and through. My husband was born in Nashville, Tennessee, and grew up in Atlanta, Georgia.

AR *What does The New Southern mean to you?* **HM** The New Southern to me is a collective awakening among creative entrepreneurs that

I hope will inspire others to be bold and live out their dreams.

AR *How do you see creativity as an important force in today's South, and the country as a whole?* **HM** Creative thought leads to a unique solution, thus disrupting industries or changing policies.

AR *What does creativity mean to you?* **HM** Creativity means endless possibilities.

AR *How does your space support your creativity?* **HM** The front of my home is my studio space! While not huge, it gets the job done and has lots of natural light. I love and obsess over colors and color theory. I also feel color in a very personal way. So it was important that the walls in my space be a blank canvas. I like to tape paper to the walls and have sketchbooks throughout my home for when inspiration strikes. My favorite ideas often happen this way.

AR *How do you feel when you're creating?* **HM** Creating art is how I synthesize and process my thoughts and emotions. When I am truly in my flow, I am possessed by my need to manifest the ideas in my brain in the physical world. There can also be times where the pressures of being a professional creative can be prohibitive to the process. That can be very challenging to work through. When I focus on creating what brings me joy, the work comes easier and the outcome is some of my best work.

AR *How do you let yourself be vulnerable enough to share your creativity?* **HM** Erykah Badu said it best: "I'm an artist. And I'm sensitive about my shit." Letting yourself be vulnerable enough to share your work can be very hard, especially when it is a very personal piece. In moments of major self-doubt, the people I trust most have encouraged me to go for it.

AR *What are some of your daily rituals?* **HM** After years of very little sleep and early mornings, I find myself enjoying slow, contemplative mornings. My husband takes our oldest two to school in the morning. It is not

"KINDNESS IS THE MOST
VALUABLE CURRENCY IN LIFE."

uncommon for me to sometimes work until 3 A.M. I am trying to shift to normal sleeping habits, but my creative energy soars at night.

AR *How did you approach the design of your space?* **HM** I approach decorating like I would starting a painting—a blank canvas with pops of color. Our kids' artwork adorns nearly every wall in our home. Since my husband and I live and work in our home with our kiddos, it is a little bit of creative chaos. We have learned to be flexible and adapt to change.

AR *Essential ingredients to produce the perfect garden party?* **HM** I love using my Aerin melamine dinnerware or eco-friendly palm-leaf plates that I can toss directly into the compost. Good food is of paramount importance at any party! Our go-to party favorites are guacamole, my husband's sliders, a charcuterie board, and lots of fresh fruit. We love fresh lemonade and sweet tea, both of which transform into the perfect spring or summer cocktail. My favorite is lemonade, club soda, and Deep Eddy's lemon or sweet tea vodka!

AR *What life pivots have you had either professionally or emotionally?* **HM** Life is constantly changing in unexpected ways. I think in some ways, as a professional creative, you get used to anticipating change. The birth of my fourth child ushered in a season of a lot of change. Following a difficult birth, some major health issues developed and I found myself really sick—Hashimoto's, celiac disease. That meant saying no to some opportunities that I would have said yes to previously. The change in pace was difficult for me, but gaining my health back took precedence. Oddly, since we have slowed our pace down, we find ourselves taking stock of everything in our lives and are more appreciative. Sometimes the world makes us feel like we have to have it all right now. You don't. Go at your own pace. Listen to your body. Rest when you need rest.

AR *Best life advice you offer, or best life advice you've received?* **HM** Genuine kindness is devoid of expecting a specific outcome. Work hard and be kind to others. It is that simple.

LEFT
Antique blue-and-white textiles paired with a classic Stark rug set the tone for Hayley's art, which depicts goddess-like, Cubist-inspired faces.

FILLER IS
THE NEW FLORAL
STYLE

FILLER ARRANGEMENT

One of my all-time favorite styling tricks (as well as a wallet-friendly option) is replacing the traditional bouquet with filler instead of tightly manicured roses or hydrangeas. This cuts out the fuss, quantitatively lasts longer (up to two months!) and is often a one-stop grocery store shop. They're also great for the holidays. There is beauty in simplicity and these arrangements help to layer in greenery, a necessary component to give life to any space. You can flat lay leaves from the grocery store and style it with bright pops of fruit like clementines or pears, or put several bunches in a vase for dramatic effect. Little sprigs on bath caddies or bedside tables can also lend an organic and soft feel to a space. These are my top filler favorites for you to incorporate into your home or any holiday tablescape. You can also bring in candlesticks to add height and layers. The goal here is keeping it pared down, classic, and achievable.

YOU WILL NEED

—

DUSTY MILLER

BABY BLUE EUCALYPTUS

ISRAELI RUSCUS

PAMPAS GRASS

BABY'S BREATH

SILVER DOLLAR EUCALYPTUS

SEEDED EUCALYPTUS

LIMONIUM

CREATIVITY IS THE NEW COMMUNITY

SUBSTANCE

Through the internet we are now connected to those who inspire us globally. Their words, their works of art, their soulful expressions become our neighboring voices, which accompany us daily over coffee or may even challenge us to dig deeper. We are bound more by our interests and creative output than our geography, political affiliations, or cultural differences. I initially viewed social media as a litmus test for my own courage as an artist. I wondered if I should share my craft, and myself, with the world. It felt scary at first, but it was also an opportunity to allow myself to be vulnerable and share the process of becoming an artist. I was open with my emotions as well as my struggles, and when I did step into that light, a beautiful community rose up around me. I view social media as a place of creativity and community rather than a place to gain an audience. Online is where I'm honest, raw, and free from my ego. As a result, I have formed deep and meaningful connections with a strong and lasting community. What I've taken away from social media is that, at end of the day, we all want to feel seen, heard, and loved.

Here are some of the ways in which I use my creativity and social media to build a community of like-minded people bound by values and mutual inspiration.

—

1 Be the light online that you want to see in the world. I remember having a really bad day. This was long before the thousands of IG friends and cross-country work trips. I realized the only thing I could control was how much love I put into the world, so I focused on where it would have the largest impact: online. The internet can be a dark place, and I find so much value combating its darkness with light and love.

2 Be open. How we experience the world is what connects us. I believe there is a direct correlation between being open and allowing magic into our lives. I'll never forget the day I shared my cancer story. At the time, I thought it was too personal and completely off topic from my photography. However, I was still healing and felt like sharing would help me. Then, someone shared their experience with cancer with me. I remember I was in my office, my dog Meyer on my lap, with tears streaming down my face. There was a courageous woman on the other side of the screen sharing her experience, and it was through creativity that we were able to have this restorative dialogue.

3 Be engaged. Studies show that inter-action, rather than voyeurism, increases our oxytocin levels. Look for the humanity rather than the likes, and the positive output will take you to places you never dreamed possible.

MINIMAL

PART 5

Thoughtfulness, intention, and mindfulness are hallmarks of the Minimal New Southern. While minimalism might seem simple, it is quite the opposite. In the pages that follow, you'll meet designers, creators, and heritage makers who have approached their spaces by sharply editing out the clutter and leaving only the essential, the striking, and the loved pieces that represent them. They've solely invited objects with great form, function, and emotional value to reside in their homes. While others might work through their ideas using a mood board, for those who subscribe to the Minimal New Southern, one object can embody their vision, a dream that might manifest years from now. Minimal spaces can often be misunderstood as cold, but it is minimalist's mindfulness in shaping their space that generates warmth, through thoughtful textures, textiles, and finishes. In a world filled with mass production and hyper-consumerism, those in this category value the quintessentially Southern tradition of singular, handmade, handcrafted goods. Instead of endless acquisition, they practice restraint, drawing on simple geometries, placement, and clean lines.

They celebrate architecture and negative space, which allow them to think, breathe, and imagine in a way that seems filled with endless possibilities.

BIOGRAPHY

—

COHOST OF NETFLIX'S *QUEER EYE*

INTERIOR DESIGNER

LIFESTYLE EXPERT

BOBBY

BERK

LOS ANGELES, CALIFORNIA

Bobby Berk's home office, featuring clean lines and a neutral color palette, is the incubator for ideas that are as magnificent as the view of the surrounding California Hills. He is a man whose passions have become his purpose and have served as a lifesaver. Growing up in a part of the country that has a tendency to be threatened by differences, he left home at fifteen years old, ending up in New York City with just a hundred dollars in his pocket. After design positions with large retailers, he landed a job at a high-end furnishing company, and with no formal training, he worked his way up to creative director. He later launched Bobby Berk Home, with locations all across the South and the East Coast. The rest is history! You likely know him as a television personality with the warmth of a close friend, but it is his grit and determination to rise above his circumstances and defy the naysayers, to become an integral part of a more tolerant culture, that makes this designer New Southern through and through.

—

AR *Tell us about yourself.* **BB** I was born in Houston, Texas, but grew up in Mount Vernon, Missouri. I've always loved design and it's been a real guiding factor in my life. I currently live in Los Angeles with my husband, Dewey, and am continuing to grow my design business while appearing on *Queer Eye*. Fun fact: I'm a total plant guy and love orchids.

AR *What ties you to the South?* **BB** There is an inherent hospitality and consideration of other people in the South. There's a real sense of kindness and humility that I relate to and love about the South. Southerners tend to have a strong loyalty to family and community, as well as a strong work ethic, so I appreciate those parts of Southern living and the people that live there.

AR *What does The New Southern mean to you?* **BB** The New Southern is about authenticity and being your best self. I think of it as a sort of casual stylishness that's rooted in creativity, community, and connection.

AR *What inspires you most about the South?* **BB** The South is filled with many intriguing parts—such historic cities, incredible nature, and welcoming people. There's definitely a distinct Southern style and I really appreciate the functionality, comfort, and viewpoint of that style.

AR *How do you think creativity unites us across political, social, and economic divides?* **BB** I think all people are inherently creative, but some have just been lucky enough to let their creativity blossom and even build their lives and careers around it. I think creativity is really at the root of the human experience and goes so much deeper than surface-level divides we might have because of politics or social or economic status.

AR *How do you see creativity as an important force in today's South, and the country as a whole?* **BB** Creativity really allows us to connect with each other on a more authentic level. Cooking is a form of creativity, and food fuels the South!

AR *What does it mean to be a creative individual in the South?* **BB** Sometimes creative individuals on the East and West Coasts get more attention than creatives in the South. So I think it's about having a real pride in where you're from and championing other local creatives, artists, makers, and designers. It's also about building on the rich history of the South and really celebrating the unique Southern point of view.

AR *How does your space support your creativity?* **BB** A space that is clean and organized really enhances my creativity. When the things around you are balanced and in place, it allows you to clear your mind of distractions and really focus on your creative endeavors.

AR *Minimal isn't boring because:*
BB minimal means that you have just what you need around you. The things you need are never boring; they are necessities.

AR *What does the Minimal New Southern mean to you, and how is this reflected in your home?* **BB** I think it's about focusing on not only style but also functionality. Selecting objects for the home that serve a purpose and look great doing it. Not being overwhelmed with the unnecessary. This is definitely an approach I take in my own home design.

AR *What is your favorite room in your house and why?* **BB** I love my kitchen. It's a real gathering point for us and a place where we can experiment with new recipes and try new things. The house is designed with the kitchen right in the center and all the rooms coming off of it, so it truly is a space for us to gather together. When I have people over to my house, we often end up in the kitchen together, so I love having it be a space that people feel really comfortable in.

AR *Describe your coffee table. What's on it, and why?* **BB** I love coffee-table books and am always finding new ones. I can't seem to stop buying them, as they not only are an endless source of inspiration for me but they make for great design accents in any space.

AR *The key to making a house a home?* **BB** Trends should never dictate the design of a home—nor do I really believe in them. Stick to your own personal style and invest in the most important pieces, building out the design from there. I'm also personally a big fan of natural materials and plants and being open to experimenting with colors and textures. At the end of the day, your home should be filled with what makes you happy, whether that be an inherited piece of furniture from your grandmother or a family photo. Fill the spaces in your home with

RIGHT
Thoughtful simplicity is the calling card of this home office. The striking geometric piece is the result of Bobby's collaboration with Leftbank Art.

objects and items that bring you joy and you'll always be happy in your own space.

AR *How are you living your best life right now?* **BB** My schedule is crazy these days. I'm constantly on a plane somewhere and am running a full-time design firm on top of everything else. I really prioritize carving out some time for myself: to exercise, cook, be outdoors, and spend time with my husband, friends, and family. It's easy to get wrapped up in the chaos of work deadlines and professional pressure, so to me, living my best life means also making time for all of the other things that make me feel happy and at peace.

AR *How do you consider yourself a courageous human?* **BB** I really strive to be my authentic self and that's something I've always worked toward. My roots were planted in New York, years after finding what I wanted home to feel like. I was on my own at a young age, which only made me be more courageous. Don't get me wrong, with courage comes a lot of doubt. While there are always parts of one's life that aren't easy, I chose to be determined to better myself and my career.

AR *How do you let yourself be vulnerable enough to share your creativity?* **BB** I learned a long time ago that not everyone is going to love everything I do, and that is OK. Being vulnerable early on in my career was harder for me. But now I realize it's just inherently a part of being a creative person: When you put your work out there, you have to be vulnerable. It comes with the territory, and if someone doesn't agree with what you do or your style, that doesn't mean that theirs is right and yours is wrong or vice versa. Creativity and design are subjective—you just have to continue to be authentically you in your designs and create.

AR *What is your personal mantra?* **BB** Never take no for an answer.

"LIVING WITH LESS IS REALLY RETURNING TO YOUR ROOTS."

BIOGRAPHY
—

FOUNDER OF THE VINTAGE VOGUE
MAKER
INTERIOR DESIGNER

CHARLOTTE BRAVO CANNON

BALTIMORE, MARYLAND

Charlotte Bravo Cannon is soft-spoken with a quiet power and a tender honesty. A self-made business owner and single mother who put herself through school while juggling being a designer, a maker, and living in her creative light, Charlotte moves through the world with nothing to prove. In her space, she celebrates simple details like the gracious knots in a wooden dresser, or floating shelves layered with lavender, geometric hung necklaces, and natural fiber art. Known for spontaneous shapes and minimal design style, the home goods she creates for the Vintage Vogue are embraced by major retailers and design mavens alike for both their form and function. They also exemplify the Minimal New Southern by embodying both warmth and tradition and a strong, clear vision and fierce individuality.

—

AR *Tell us about yourself.* CBC The prologue of my story begins in the South. More south than the South, in South America. To be more specific, I am a first-generation American born to Afro-Colombian parents. When I turned ten, my mother became a single mom and our sometimes-unstable home life took me to eleven different schools throughout Florida and Arizona. By the time I was twenty-one, I had two small children, worked full-time, and attended college full-time. It took seven years to complete my degree in interior architecture. After doing design work in public rec spaces and senior living facilities, I decided I needed to reclaim the creativity that was being stifled in my nine-to-five. This was the birth of the Vintage Vogue. Out of my little creative studio, I sold modern decor for the home that was purchased by companies like West Elm and Madewell and countless boutiques in the US and around the world. By 2017, I decided to return to my roots in interior architecture and now work full-time as a designer in a high-end residential design firm. The Vintage Vogue still lives, but in one-of-a-kind pieces and experimental projects.

AR *What does The New Southern mean to you?* CBC I see the movement as one that coalesces character and individuality with the richness of tradition. It embraces a fresh and updated aesthetic while retaining warmth and hospitality.

AR *What inspires you most about the South?* CBC Here in Baltimore in particular, I'm inspired by the reinvention I see all around me, both within the people and the city itself. There's a push by individuals to be seen as they are and to create a city with its own vibe. I love being part of that energy.

AR *How do you think creativity unites us across political, social, and economic divides?* CBC The beauty of creativity is that it comes from the soul. It is born of a deep, instinctual space. I think because it originates in a pure place, it has power, and that power can rise above all the issues that divide us because we all desire to be truly touched from within. Art is a form of love, and love heals everything.

AR *How do you see creativity as an important force in today's South, and the country as a whole?* CBC The future belongs to those who can create—those who can create a new vision in the midst of so much heartache in the world. We need those who are bold enough to be vulnerable enough to bare their souls and share their creative light even in the face of rejection, be it here in the South, or in the United States at large.

AR *How did you approach the design of your space?* CBC My home came as a result of my separation. I was seeking out a space for myself, my sixteen-year-old daughter, and my fourteen-year-old son where we could find peace and retreat to a quiet space amid our shifting reality. I am naturally drawn to a minimal aesthetic, but here, in this place with everything that I have juggled throughout the last several months, it was especially crucial to be at peace. I find that peace in monochromatic spaces and an abundance of negative space.

AR *What's your motto behind living with less?* CBC I want to move about the world as freely as possible, no baggage. I don't want to have to hold on to anything I'm not meant to keep; that's too much wasted energy. If I have an issue with you, let's address it. If I have a

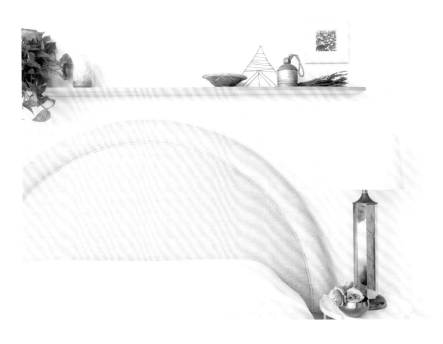

messy desk, let me clear it off so I can breathe and work efficiently. If I live with fewer things mentally and materially, then I am free to seek out and walk in my purpose.

AR *What does the Minimal New Southern mean to you and how is this reflected in your home?* **CBC** I am not encumbered by anyone's prejudices about the kind of person I am. I am not stagnant. I can reinvent myself and each day make a conscious decision who I want to be. My home reflects this in that it is a clean slate. I haven't imposed an identity onto it. It is pared down to its essentials with sentimental flourishes here and there, but, ultimately, the people that I bring into it and the memories that are shared there are what I hold dear.

AR *Minimal isn't boring because:* **CBC** of the clarity it provides me to fully embrace the most important things in my life.

AR *What is your favorite room in your house?* **CBC** My bedroom. The corner windows face south and east so the light at all times of the day is killer. I feel immediately regenerated when I lie on my bed and the sunlight washes over me.

AR *How does your space support your creativity?* **CBC** The freshness of light and airiness lends a sense of optimism and peace to my home. Both are essential for me to get into a creative state of mind.

AR *How do you feel when you're creating?* **CBC** I feel blessed and also empowered.

It's a deep spiritual connection, where in that moment of creating something beautiful I feel like I've been touched with a unique gift that is special only to me and only I can express it. It is gratitude materialized.

AR *How are you living your best life right now?* **CBC** By being mindful of this moment. It is a sacred and tenuous space that I don't ever want to take for granted. I value quietness and restfulness, and that renews me to pursue every day with gratitude and passion.

AR *How do you consider yourself a courageous human?* **CBC** I am a courageous human because I am wholeheartedly convinced life is beautiful and the life I live reflects that. I choose to laugh even when pieces of me hurt. I choose to find those icky parts of me that I'm not proud of, bring them to the surface, and nourish them to a healthy state. I choose to share what light I have with others as often as possible. I choose, and to choose is to be courageous.

AR *What is your personal mantra?* **CBC** "The key to happiness is the decision to be happy." This is a quote from Marianne Williamson that I have meditated on for over a year now. We have so much power as human beings. The power to shape our reality is in our hands. I will be hit and maybe down for the count for a time, but ultimately, I can come back to being at peace, to being full of life. Every thought I have has tremendous implications, and I don't ever want to take that for granted.

"THE FUTURE BELONGS
TO THOSE WHO CAN CREATE."

BIOGRAPHY

—

EDUCATOR
FOUNDER OF THE ABODE AND NOMAD COLLECTIVE
PHOTOGRAPHER

BROOKE MORGAN

NASHVILLE, TENNESSEE

While her first passion was education, Brooke Morgan took a leap of faith when she followed another one of her interests, her passion for handmade goods, launching Nomad Collective, a global lifestyle brand supporting artists from around the world. Brooke procures her wares from indigenous female-driven tribes and then sells them in Nashville. Her new communal gathering and ceremonial event space, the Abode, reflects her commitment to pieces with a story. In this minimal space, with clean lines that make it feel light and airy, there is great depth to be experienced in individual moments, through the substance and history of the pieces she's intentionally chosen for it. With a quiet yet powerful femininity, her living room is designed for gathering with long benches, an L-shaped couch, and a coffee table low to the ground to invite sitting on the unfinished wood floors. The journals on the table serve as nods to a rich old Southern written tradition, while the bathroom speaks to bringing in the outdoors in unexpected, Minimal New Southern ways. She also has no chairs at the head of her dining table, to send a purposeful, egalitarian message. Mostly though, her space is balanced with necessity and a grounding intention emblematic of Minimal New Southern living.

—

AR *What ties you to the South?* BM My roots. My grandparents were born and raised in Kentucky and East Tennessee. I was born and raised in Texas, but moved to Nashville for college. I've considered leaving a thousand times, but these hills are in my bloodline, and this feels like home.

AR *What does The New Southern mean to you?* BM Moving forward, paring down, building bridges, honoring nature as the great source of all wisdom, slow organic movement, open-mindedness, equanimity, and acceptance.

AR *What inspires you most about the South?* BM Its warmth and lush green hills,

the seasons, its resilience and its paradoxes, its immigrants.

AR *How do you think creativity unites us across political, social, and economic divides?* BM Art is the great equalizer. That's why Nomad Collective was born, as a way to honor the creativity of all people, regardless of demographics or context, as something that is both fundamentally human and fundamentally divine. It is God in all of us, regardless of race, class, gender, and the other artificial divisions of society. We are all creators at the core because the great Creator is our core.

AR *How do you see creativity as an important force in today's South, and the country as a whole?* BM Creativity is not a luxury or a superficial pursuit. It is imperative, especially in an age in which so many entities are doing the thinking and the feeling for us as a society. For us to move forward, individually and collectively, we must ask ourselves, "What needs to die so that new life can be born?"

AR *What drew you to your space?* BM I have been drawn to rustic adobes for a long time, for their primitive, down-to-earth, global quality. And honestly, the stars aligned for my son and I to make this one our home base. It's in a burgeoning area in East Nashville, tucked away on a charming street.

AR *What is your design philosophy?* BM My basic philosophy is that a space is first and foremost a reflection of the people inside. Function and flow are foundational. Also letting the story lead—home is the storybook of our lives. How does the space make you feel? Most important question to ask. The body knows. And aesthetics are just a vehicle for meaningful connection, creativity, and well-being.

AR *How is the Minimal New Southern reflected in your home?* BM It means being open, fine-tuning the details, bringing the outside in, allowing space and breath, and honoring all who enter as my own flesh and blood. The Abode has a feeling, an energy. Beyond aesthetics, it's a place of peace, comfort, creativity, and healing. The design elements—such as texture, softness, arches, a natural palette, minimalism, and original art—are just vessels for communicating the deeper values.

AR *Describe your coffee table.* **BM** My coffee table is an antique Japanese tea table, clad with melted candles, art books, and a hand-made leather guestbook with the signatures of everyone who enters here—because I can't live without light, art, and people.

AR *What is your personal color palette?* **BM** Colors of the earth—rust, dusty sienna, deep browns, charcoal, olive green, eucalyptus, cream, navy blue.

AR *What is the key to making a house a home?* **BM** Soul. More story, less stuff. More nature, less polish. Authenticity over aesthetic. Wabi-sabi.

AR *What are your daily rituals?* **BM** Coffee and prayer on a floor pillow each morning, unless my son rises early. I try to read and write every day, preferably in the morning. As a teacher, it's tough, because my day starts so early, but I carve out pockets of time to nurture this as I'm able. Tea in the afternoon is becoming a ritual that I have grown to love.

AR *What does creativity mean to you?* **BM** Death and rebirth, continual evolution, movement. Traditional nomads depend on movement to survive, and I really believe that we all do. We are never finished, we are beautifully imperfect, and this is the essence of creativity.

AR *How do you consider yourself a courageous human?* **BM** It takes courage to

listen to the truth, the quiet voice within, and live it out with abandon. I tend to live in denial, avoiding negative emotions for the sake of others. I become preoccupied with avoiding pain and conflict, so my current practice of courage is to sit with discomfort and speak difficult truths in love, to state my needs, even at the risk of hurting someone. Peace is my compass, and I'm finding that true courage lies in being still, in waiting, in sitting with groundlessness and the in-between. Life has given me courage when I needed it most, but for me, the greatest challenge is receiving it.

AR *What life pivots have you had either professionally or emotionally?* **BM** My business has been a great metaphor for my life. At first, I was trying so hard to hustle and make it happen, for the "right people" to see it and give it a thumbs up. I wanted to arrive, to be recognized, and there was little joy in the journey. After a number of trials and errors, I started to loosen my grip. I stopped trying to control everything, and only within the last year or two have I really let it go and have a life of its own. Now it's really starting to fly in a direction that I could not have manifested on my own. The same is true in all facets of my life—there is great power in letting go, in getting out of the way. I've learned that it's easier to let go and find true joy than to hang on to what feels safe and comfortable but is actually killing our spirit. Fear is an illusion, something to be cradled and caressed. We can walk straight through it, fall to the floor, and get up again. I've learned life has so much more to give us than we can take from it, and only the failures can teach, transform, and give us true joy. As many wiser have said, the only way up, really, is down.

"IF YOU DON'T LOVE IT, LET IT GO."

BIOGRAPHY
—

JAMES SAAVEDRA DESIGN STUDIO
INTERIOR DESIGNER
SOULFUL SPIRIT

JAMES SAAVEDRA

AUSTIN, TEXAS

"THE THINGS PEOPLE CREATE ARE THE DIARIES OF THEIR LIVES."

A true maker at heart, James Saavedra is a deeply spiritual person who values quality over quantity. Despite the South's polarizing past, it has always had a deep beauty that emanates from its tradition of making, and James embodies this heritage. With pieces like the bed frame he fashioned from knotty plywood purchased inexpensively at Home Depot as well as his forthcoming line of modern heritage home goods, it's clear that he loves through his hands and celebrates the materials and architectural details. In just nine hundred square feet, he has created an intentional space filled with warmth and clean lines. Starting with a gallery-like white box, his home demonstrates a style that values juxtaposition with nods to nature. Utilizing asymmetry and floating shelves, as well as a multitude of textures, James considers placement, shape, and scale to make his rooms feel like pieces of meditative, modern art on canvas.

—

AR *Tell us about yourself.* **JS** I am a designer of deceptively simple spaces as well as deeply personal handmade furnishings and objects. I believe in the beauty of imperfection, and that the things people create are the diaries of their lives. I think there's true heart in a good home-cooked meal, and that love is a quality that you can definitely serve up on a plate. I'm constantly creating objects of beauty, and my passion right now is figuring out how to connect the dots between creating beautiful environments and modern heritage belongings and being of service.

AR *What ties you to the South?* **JS** I am a California boy, born and raised. On the surface, I am tied to the South simply because of an impulse decision to relocate to someplace new, but, in hindsight, my time spent in the South has tied me to discovering the most authentic version of myself—exploring purpose and reigniting creative passions still to be explored.

AR *What does The New Southern mean to you?* **JS** The New Southern is a movement of authenticity, fierce creativity, and the graciousness found in a community that is pursuing their passions and disrupting the old way of "doing business." I am constantly finding awe and inspiration in others who are following their passions and using it to inspire and uplift others.

AR *What inspires you most about the South?* **JS** There's a magic combination here where good old-fashioned perseverance meets charm and a gesture of kindness. There is an abundance of creative pursuit of passion.

AR *How do you think creativity unites us across political, social, and economic divides?* **JS** For myself, the exchange of creativity is created and received at the emotional level. Despite divergent experiences or beliefs, everyone has these remarkable gifts of imagination and emotion. It's the reason why a painting created by a stranger we will never know can stop us in our tracks with awe or songs can make us weep. Creativity exists beyond barriers. And what I know for sure is that all human beings are creative beings.

AR *How do you see creativity as an important force in today's South, and the country*

ABOVE
The work of fine art landscape photographer Todd McPhetridge adds visual depth within this all-white space. A minimal pendant designed by CB2 collaborator Andrew Neyer takes center stage in the kitchen.

LEFT
Inspired by both Donald Judd and modest materials, James designed and built a bed made from unfinished plywood from Home Depot.

as a whole? JS Here in the South, and in the country as a whole, I see a return to the maker's movement across all platforms. There are people who are harnessing their creativity to create something new and innovate in the digital space, just as there are those who are expressing their creativity with the things that they make with their hands. Creativity is the starting point of innovation. Every great brand or impactful movement began as just an idea. We are built on a foundation of creative ideas and creative people that find ways to see new opportunities to improve, innovate, and disrupt.

AR *What is your general home-design philosophy?* JS As with any of the spaces I design, I start with the feeling, and I am sure this sounds a bit woo-woo, but I really listen to the space, and what happens next is like a download from the ether. Once I have the feel for the space, I ruthlessly edit out what's not necessary and eliminate as much visual clutter as possible. My natural inclination is to build a space around clean lines that allow shape and form to shine, to implement expertly crafted details that appear deceptively simple, and to layer and contrast natural textures that invite you to interact and experience the space. This combination creates a sense of gravity and ease that can be breathtaking in its simplicity.

AR *How does this philosophy reflect in your life?* JS I believe that is also true in life—we want a sense of gravity, i.e., purpose that feels authentic and can be expressed with natural ease. I apply this approach to most everything I do—how do I perfect the best X without overcomplicating the end result.

AR *Describe your coffee table.* JS The coffee table is a design by John Saladino from 1976. It appeared in *House Beautiful*. Coming up in design, I have always admired Saladino's work, so finding this table was a lucky discovery. It is a perfect example of what I gravitate toward—natural materials, simple lines, striking presence.

AR *How does your space support your creativity?* JS My home, like my design work, is a reflection of who I am. It's filled with furniture and objects I have designed, which remind me of the simple beauty I strive to cultivate. It is purposefully edited and has minimal visual clutter, which allows me the freedom to think, to meditate, and to imagine. Most importantly, it feels authentic, and when that happens, there is a sense of ease that allows you to simply be in your space.

AR *How do you consider yourself a courageous human?* JS Courage isn't about going through life without fear. Courage is the willingness to feel deeply, live fully, and speak authentically. Courage isn't an event—it's a practice. Some days are easier than others, but I believe that in the trying, I am already courageous.

COFOUNDER OF THE HOME EDIT
NEW YORK TIMES BESTSELLING AUTHOR
CHAMPAGNE CONNOISSEUR

CLEA
SHEARER

NASHVILLE, TENNESSEE

The kaleidoscope of color found in Clea Shearer's space is a brilliant display of home editing at its best. From her pantries to her books, the rainbow of color coordination celebrates organization and function. As for the rest of the house, it's black and white all the way down to the hides. There is warmth found in the personal touches, like her fashion-pioneer grandmother's glasses, which are housed in a black-and-white shadow box alongside original photographs of artists such as Bob Dylan taken by her talented husband, John Shearer. Clea and her business partner Joanna Teplin's organization system fits right in with The New Southern and helps busy homeowners incorporate an efficient sorting method that saves time and allows space for success in other endeavors. And by fostering a life governed by order and flow, Clea opens the door for more time spent with loved ones, filled with beautiful, uncluttered moments.

—

AR *Tell us about yourself.* **CS** I'm a control freak, a neat freak, an overachiever, an over-thinker, a perfectionist, a doer, a maker, a helper, but most importantly, I am authentically —and unapologetically—myself.

AR *What ties you to the South?* **CS** I moved to the South for my husband's job but ended up establishing my own company, the Home Edit, which is based in Nashville. We owe our current success to the warmth and inclusive nature of our city.

AR *What does The New Southern mean to you?* **CS** I had a lot of preconceived notions about the South prior to moving here in 2015. So, to me, the "new" South is the South I see every day that continues to surprise and inspire me. The endless stream of new restaurants and hotels making their home in Nashville, the incredible design aesthetic we see in so many homes, the live music, and so much more.

AR *How do you think creativity unites us across political, social, and economic divides?* **CS** Art is the great equalizer since it takes on all forms. Creativity requires no formal education or training and can transcend all divides.

AR *How do you see creativity as an important force in today's South, and the country as a whole?* **CS** I can only speak for myself, but I think Nashville gave me the space and freedom to create something for myself. I don't think it could have been possible in another city. The culture, the pace of life, the open-mindedness, the inclusivity—it all allowed me to flourish.

AR *What is your general home-design philosophy?* **CS** My home-design philosophy is black and white, contemporary without being overly traditional or overly modern, clean lines and right angles, and the occasional touch of greenery. My kids' bedrooms and the playroom are on the second floor, so for them, I allow the full spectrum of the rainbow. I try to keep our home clutter-free so our items are relatively minimal, and everything is contained in its place.

LEFT
Clea's signature aesthetic— white, black, and rainbow —appears throughout the home.

BELOW
The kid's playroom (left) also features a friendly reminder that is very much in line with Clea's approach to living in beautiful, uncluttered spaces. A sentimental nook (right) in Clea's house displays her legendary grandmother's glasses, her grandfather's camera collection, and the table number from her wedding.

LEFT
An original portrait of Bob Dylan by Clea's husband, John Shearer, and artwork by Southern artist Chris Coleman tie into the black-and-white color palette of the home.

AR *Describe your signature aesthetic in three words.* **CS** Black, white, and rainbow.

AR *What is your favorite room in your house?* **CS** My dining room. It's bright and light and has a mile-long view of trees out the window.

AR *Describe your coffee table.* **CS** Only greenery. I like to keep it clean and pile-free.

AR *The key to making a house a home?* **CS** I'm not a good example of making a house homey. My ideal aesthetic is "does anyone actually live here?" I think less is best so I get rid of anything that isn't in constant use.

AR *Minimal isn't boring because:* **CS** simplicity is timeless and never out of style.

AR *How does your space support your creativity?* **CS** I can't think with clutter and messes, so keeping everything minimal allows me to focus on everything else.

AR *What does it mean to be a creative individual in the South?* **CS** Hardworking, forward thinking, constantly evolving.

AR *How do you feel when you're creating?* **CS** Exhilarated and proud.

AR *What does creativity mean to you?* **CS** It means coming up with a solution to a problem someone else can't solve.

AR *What are your daily rituals?* **CS** Stomping around the house telling my husband and kids that I'm going to throw their stuff away if they don't move it to their room or office.

AR *What life pivots have you had either professionally or emotionally?* **CS** Moving to Nashville was an unexpected and enormous life change, but it worked.

AR *What is your personal mantra?* **CS** Surviving not thriving—and sometimes—thriving, but not surviving.

AR *How are you living your best life right now?* **CS** I don't know if I'd say it's my "best" life, but it's the life I have and I'm grateful for it. It's hard juggling a successful business and a family, but I do the best I can and that's good enough for me.

AR *Best life advice you offer, or best life advice you've received?* **CS** "Never accept the first hotel room they give you"—my mother.

BIOGRAPHY

—

FOUNDER OF ELIZABETH SUZANN
INTENTIONAL CLOTHING DESIGNER

ELIZABETH PAPE

NASHVILLE, TENNESSEE

RIGHT
The warehouse of Elizabeth's
clothing manufacturing
company is designed to
encourage a communal
work culture rooted in
kindness by showcasing
such elements as Nashville's
poster initiative against hate
and discrimination.

Elizabeth Pape has created a work culture rooted in kindness, acceptance, and love. Traditionally in the South, women often wear bright colors, florals, and stiff fabrics, but when a woman wears clothes designed by Elizabeth, the minimal colors and utter breathability of the garments allow the wearer's confidence to shine as her most valuable accessory. Architecturally clean and a celebration of the beauty in simplicity, Elizabeth's clothes are much like the space in which they're created. Both are designed with every woman, every size, and every walk of life in mind. Her light-filled warehouse, with mismatched chairs, old Southern-wood tables, and painted wall florals from Nashville-based artist Emily Leonard, is meant for communal working, and the handmade, hand-dyed nature of her clothing speaks to a maker heritage. The dichotomy between the softness of the organic linen, silk, and cotton she's working with set against the hard concrete surfaces of her space reminds us that there are those who use their gifts and their hands to create soft things that make life easier for us all in a world that might otherwise feel much less comfortable.

—

AR *Tell us about yourself.* EP I own a clothing design and manufacturing company in Nashville, Tennessee. We make really good products and we do it the right way. I love my work immensely, and when I'm not working, I like to enjoy time with my family and dogs. I'm a total homebody, and my favorite kind of night is one spent at home with a delicious meal, comfy pajamas, and a good movie.

AR *What ties you to the South?* EP I was born in North Carolina and both my parents were raised there. I grew up in various cities throughout the southeast: Wilmington, North Carolina; Greenville, North Carolina; Roanoke, Virginia; and the Florida Keys.

AR *What does The New Southern mean to you?* EP To me, the term represents a reclaiming. The South has a history filled with

pain, struggle, and oppression for marginalized communities, and I'm a part of that system. But there is honor in reclaiming what it means to be Southern and committing to the lifelong work of unraveling injustice here. There are many things I love and admire about this part of the country, and the term *New Southern* feels like a way to take the best aspects of this region and let them motivate and shape what our communities here could look like in years to come.

AR *What inspires you most about the South?* EP The ease and comfort. When I think of the South, I think of home, and I think of comfort. Food that brings me joy and makes me feel loved, homes filled with softness and warmth, long hugs from family members. As a region, I think we prioritize comfort over things like image or success, and I haven't found that in other cities I've visited.

AR *How do you think creativity unites us across political, social, and economic divides?* EP Creativity is a common language. We may not share the same perspective, taste, or life experience, but all humans have innate creativity and know what it's like to marvel in something that came from our own two hands. Whether it's a formal piece of artwork or a simple weeknight meal, we can connect over the joy of creation.

AR *How do you see creativity as an important force in today's South, and the country as a whole?* EP I think creativity is critical everywhere, but in the South, I see an exciting revival of heritage art forms like quilting, woodworking, and weaving. It is really cool to see crafts that were necessary life skills one hundred years ago become valued and celebrated as creative endeavors. The respect and recognition of creative work that used to fall under the umbrella of domestic work is so powerful, and shines a light on the art women in particular bring to every aspect of life.

AR *What is your general design philosophy?* EP My general philosophy is to follow a

few guiding principles: Keep it simple, prioritize natural light, use plants to add life, add warmth through natural materials, and aim for synchronicity to reduce visual stress.

AR *Minimal isn't boring because:* EP it's personal and totally unique to you. Minimal isn't an aesthetic, it's not having an all-cream-and-beige home, or only wearing black turtlenecks—it's going to look different for each individual. It's about identifying what things in your life are truly essential to your happiness and investing in those things deeply rather than diluting your time, energy, and money by spending them on things that are less important to you.

AR *What's your motto behind living with less?* EP As much as I can, I try to not let my life get bigger than it needs to be. It's not easy, and the bar is different for everyone, but restraining myself and keeping things simple contributes to my happiness and peace daily. The more objects that are in my life, the more mental space and energy they require. I can feel myself slipping into "management mode," where I get busy just maintaining all the "things" in my life, and that is always a sign that I need to scale back and reevaluate my habits.

AR *How do you let yourself be vulnerable enough to share your creativity?* EP I don't always. There are some ideas that feel too fragile to be shared, and if they weren't received well, it would break my heart. But I'm in a unique position in that in my design work I have to share my ideas with my team because they are the ones that bring them to life for customers. I can't release a product without first sharing it with our whole team, so I just have to go for it. Often I have workshopped the idea or gotten

LEFT
The towering Emily Leonard abstract painting evokes softness in this Minimal New Southern space.

feedback throughout the process, so it's a bit easier that way. And then when it's time to share a new idea with the public, I've already broken the ice with our team and I have that whole support system. The step-by-step process is really helpful for me.

AR *How do you consider yourself a courageous human?* EP I don't know that I am exceptionally courageous, but I would say that my most courageous quality is my ability to work hard. I commit to bold objectives (the committing is the part that sounds courageous, but that's actually the easy part) and then do my absolute best to get things done regardless of personal cost.

AR *What is your personal mantra?* EP "It will be fine." Everyone around me knows I say this all the time, and it's almost always true. Everything might not be great, it might not be easy, but it will be fine. Things have a way of working out, and humans are strong and resilient—so I try to remember, and remind others, that we'll find a way to get through most things and end up OK.

AR *How are you living your best life right now?* EP By taking things one day at a time, reminding myself that—while looking toward the next mile marker is critical—life is made up of the time spent in the metaphorical car, not the signs on the side of the road telling us where we are. Enjoying each day moment by moment is a practice I'm working on!

AR *Best life advice you offer, or the best life advice you've received?* EP You cannot do anything well if you are trying to do everything. Pick what matters most to you and give those things your all.

"IT'S ABOUT IDENTIFYING WHAT THINGS IN YOUR LIFE ARE TRULY ESSENTIAL TO YOUR HAPPINESS."

SUSPENDED CEILING ART IS
THE NEW GALLERY WALL

STYLE

YOU WILL NEED

—

2 COBRA CEILING DRILLERS
2 THIN D-RINGS
THIN CABLE WIRE
SPRAY PAINT

This can be done anywhere you want to create an unexpected focal point. I find living rooms and bedrooms are a great place to experiment, as seen within my home on pages 26-27. All you need is a screwdriver, about thirty dollars, and five simple steps to make your art soar.

—

1 Measure the width of your frame and screw two Cobra Ceiling Drillers (360-degree-swivel flush-mount ceiling hooks) into the ceiling the frame's width apart. **2** Attach two small D-rings on the back of your frame (one on each side), if they are not already there. I like to place my D-rings as close to the top of the frame as possible without them showing. **3** Spray the wire with the spray paint and allow to dry. I recommend choosing the same color spray paint as your drapes or wall to help the wire blend into the background color and create a floating effect.
4 Measure and cut wire to have frame hang at eye level. Create a loop at one end of the wire and wrap the other end of the wire around the D-ring attached to the frame. Repeat for second wire. **5** Hang the loop end of the wire on the Cobra hooks attached to the ceiling. **6** Once hung, if there are any color inconsistencies, spray a paper towel with the spray paint and hand dab the color to adhere to the wire.

I believe how we display art is just as important as the art itself. As a photographer with a sensitive eye, I like my gaze to travel around the room without any obvious disruptions of flow. When the scale is off, items in the room are competing rather than communicating. Ceiling art is a quick and inexpensive way to blend a room together while still making a statement. Floating pieces in front of drapery panels go together like cowboy boots and Nashville!

MANIFESTING IS
THE NEW DAYDREAMING

SUBSTANCE

We spend almost half of our waking hours daydreaming. When we daydream, we detach from our external environment and our attention moves inward. It is a passive state, almost a stream of consciousness, in which we start to imagine how our lives could be different. In contrast, manifesting is a more active state of mind that takes daydreaming to the next level to help us actualize our goals and to up-level our dreams. When we manifest, we bring the same thoughtfulness and intention that characterize the ethos of the Minimal New Southern. The idea is anything is possible—if you can see it in your mind's eye, you can transform it into a reality. To do this, you need to seek out what I call the "negative space."

The negative space is the space in between, the place where there is room to breathe, the place where we can hear our thoughts, the place where we can recognize our innermost desires and open up to ideas for the future. It is the space to generate your own ingenuity and drive. We live in the most visually stimulating time in history, and negative space provides a sense of relief to help us produce, gain clarity, and see how our inspirations may better the world around us. Once you have found this space within you, I encourage you to set a clear intention: Think about what your goal or dream is and what is motivating it. Dreams motivated by ego-driven measures, such as money or status, are not as powerful as the dreams that involve self-actualization and achieving our fullest potential. Then visualize and feel all the steps that must happen to make your dream a reality. The details matter here. Visualize the initial steps, take stock in what it feels like to start moving forward, and let yourself be the architect of the vision by writing down these details. Equally important is recognizing and acknowledging any limiting beliefs. Actively dismantle the self-dialogue holding you back. Tell yourself that you are worthy of your dreams, be grateful for the process, and feel what it feels like as if it were already a reality. Repeat this process over time. Dreams are manifested by making changes, creating new daily habits, and saying yes to the things that align with the future vision you are creating for yourself and others. A simple question to ask yourself: Is this in alignment with my vision and how does this support a greater good?

In my case, my dream was to publish a book that would inspire the hearts and minds of those who read it. I would visualize each step of the process, from working with the literary agent who supported my vision, to writing the book proposal, to flying to New York for meetings, to the bid day with publishers, to signing a contract in my attorney's office, to celebrating with my husband over dinner, to submitting the final manuscript, and lastly holding my book in my hands and sharing it with The New Southern community.

I invite you to give yourself permission to create space for yourself, to stare at the negative space this white wall provides, and to see the possibilities your dreams hold. Manifest here.

PLAYFUL

PART 6

Turn up the music. Fire up the grill. Slide on your heart-shaped neon sunglasses and get ready to play. The spirited spaces in this chapter are the design equivalent of a night bellied up to the bar, shamelessly flirting. Fun and quirky, whimsical and seductive, charismatic and rebellious, these spaces have personality to spare. In the pages that follow, you'll find bookshelves bursting with every color of the rainbow, a hulking chromatic pop art painting of Bill Murray lording over a living room, and walls painted with hues so fierce that spaces are transformed into an energizing sensory experience.

The Playful New Southerners featured here make their own rules daily. They're the ones with vinyl record collections and vintage jumpsuits who joyfully express themselves while inviting you to be creative and dream alongside them. The cool kids live and work in these spaces—boss-lady chefs, free-spirit wanderers, tech mavens. They draw from the cultural richness of the Southern landscape around them, ranging from music to food to handcrafted art, and they're turning convention on its head. Mostly though, they're connected to their own spirituality and to the others around them. The ability to see awe and wonder in the world and to simply play without purpose is often lost as we get older, but it still burns bright in the souls of this crowd. They dance like no one's watching and embrace their creative childlike freedom. With a little imagination and lots of heart, turn the page and come dream with us.

BIOGRAPHY

—

JUDGE ON FOOD NETWORK'S *CHOPPED*
JAMES BEARD AWARD WINNER
RESTAURATEUR
CHEF
AUTHOR

MANEET CHAUHAN

NASHVILLE, TENNESSEE

Maneet Chauhan doesn't believe in balance. Instead, she promised herself a long time ago that each moment would get 100 percent of her attention. She lives in the present, not consumed by the moments that just passed or the thoughts of tomorrow. She feels there is no way to do this without an incredible support system, and hers is made up of her husband, her kids, and the people she works with daily. She also believes that inspiration is everywhere—whether it comes from her patrons, sous chefs, or dishwashers. It is this passion and drive that has enabled her to create a restaurant vibrating with saturated color, teeming with teal and multicolored bangle bracelets, and also exuding a casual warmth that matches her vivacious and warm personality.

Maneet has woven herself, and her dreams, into the changing Southern tapestry, always pushing forward to create, produce, love, grow, and cook. This is why she represents the perfect collision of tradition and the New Southern, through preserving the idea that food and love bring people together, and marrying it with the idea that dining should be experiential. Her restaurants deliver this full package, made possible by a talented, gracefully empowered boss lady.

—

AR *Tell us about yourself.* **MC** I have learned over the years that you need to enjoy whatever you are doing, so right now I am absolutely enjoying life, family, and work.

AR *What ties you to the South?*
MC Moving to the South actually happened to us—it wasn't planned. It was really interesting because we were living in New York. Vivek, my husband, had a couple of restaurants in New York. Chauhan Ale & Masala was my first venture. And the first thing about the South was that, oh my God, everything takes so long. In the South you learn patience. So the

project of building our new restaurant took an extra year. Along the way, we found out that we were expecting baby number two, and our son was born three months early—he was a twenty-six-weeker and he was two-and-a-half pounds, lighter than a gallon of milk—and I think what really endeared us to the South, or made us true Southerners, was the way the entire city embraced us, was there for us, and supported us. So many things about the South remind me of where I grew up. It's the soul of the people—how warm and welcoming people are.

AR *What does The New Southern mean to you?* **MC** The New Southern means the expansion of culture and cuisine. The South has been one of the most diverse regions cuisine-wise because of the melting pot of different cultural influences. That pot is becoming bigger as more and more groups come in and make the South their home.

AR *What inspires you most about the South?* **MC** How it came to be and how it's evolved. I want to make sure that it keeps evolving and getting better for everyone.

AR *What does the Playful New Southern mean to you and how is this reflected in your restaurants?* **MC** Playful means not taking things too seriously. That's reflected in my restaurants with the play on color and textures.

AR *How did you approach the design of your restaurant Chaatable?* **MC** It was a blank canvas, and that was a great starting point for us. My husband and I both grew up in India and wanted the space to be like stepping into India for the first time—a true journey for the senses. Everything is bright, vibrant, and colorful. My design philosophy is that functionality is key, but there has to be a generous dose of drama. There must be a wow factor. When people come into a restaurant, they're expecting an experience. It's our responsibility to provide that experience.

"THE NEW SOUTHERN MEANS THE
EXPANSION OF CULTURE AND CUISINE."

LEFT
Maneet's fourth restaurant
concept Chaatable is a
journey for the senses,
introducing Indian street-
food cuisine to Nashville.
Vibrant Bollywood posters,
hanging lanterns, energizing
color themes, and meals
meant for sharing are
beautiful forces inspiring
The New Southern tapestry.

AR *How do you think creativity unites us across political, social, and economic divides?* **MC** Creativity is a humbling trait that sees no barriers, uniting us all as people.

AR *What is your personal mantra?* **MC** My mantra in life is: "Nothing ventured, nothing gained." It is with me today, and I am talking about twenty years—twenty years of how that saying has subconsciously made its presence in my very existence and being. It is something which I am constantly repeating—constantly. I think that it is up to a person themselves to make that shift.

AR *How are you living your best life right now?* **MC** I always live my best life! I've been blessed with amazing opportunities—to travel and meet new people. Plus, my family and I love our life here in the South.

AR *Best life advice you offer, or best life advice you've received?* **MC** Do whatever you want to do, but be the best at it. Also, the most valuable advice I can give is to learn from your mistakes, because they are the biggest, most valuable lessons in life. I think the new generation of strong women that we are seeing are standing here because there are so many women before us who dared to dream. And I come from India, where the depth of daring to dream is so much deeper there than over here, but they dared. They were the fearless ones. I almost think that we got the easy way out.

BIOGRAPHY

—

COFOUNDER OF A BEAUTIFUL MESS,
A COLOR STORY AND FILMM APPS
FORBES HOME INFLUENCER
AUTHOR

ELSIE LARSON

NASHVILLE, TENNESSEE

Elsie Larson's cheerful, airy, and bright home defines retro playful. From the teal floors and pink doors to the rainbow-colored book collection she spent years compiling, she is a master at making thoughtful, edited rooms appear effortless. She also seamlessly updates old Southern concepts like wicker rattan and wallpaper by choosing modern designs and whimsical patterns to infuse her space with creative energy. As a veteran blogger turned app developer, she believes it's important that as her career evolves, her home gets updates too. Though, in a unique and beautiful twist, the pièce de résistance of Elsie's home is actually her daughters' playroom. Bursting with color, the room has a dedicated space for crafting, promoting creativity and unrestrained exploration in her daughters' every day. This is something Elsie's mother did with her as a child, and it was important to Elsie to pass it down. Elsie has unwavering dedication to teaching her daughters that we're all interconnected creative beings, regardless of skin color, religion, or socioeconomic status. It is this concept—which we all yearn to create as humans—that permeates her home and challenges convention.

—

AR *Tell us about yourself.* EL I believe in creating a life you're excited to live every day. That includes the home. My home isn't the fanciest or most expensive home, but it's my dream home because I spent years pouring love and energy into customizing every nook and corner. The outcome of all that effort is so much joy every day. I made a place I love to be. In my free time, I love shopping at flea markets, my favorite guilty pleasures are pasta and Jeni's ice cream, and I'll drop anything to cuddle with my little girl.

AR *What ties you to the South?* EL I have lived in Nashville for four years. My husband is a songwriter and producer, so we moved here for his career. I love it too, and my career has grown since living here as well.

AR *What does The New Southern mean to you?* EL That Southern people want to be able to create their own definition and let go of past stereotypes. My experience of the people in Nashville has been as loving, progressive, accepting, and open-minded.

AR *What does it mean to be a creative individual in the South?* EL I think that since I live in the South, it's more important than ever to be vocal about what I believe in. I don't participate in call-out culture and I don't believe that shaming people with different beliefs leads to real change. I do believe in having real, sometimes awkward, conversations. The kind that makes your heart beat fast sometimes. I think that being open and honest about what I believe is the best example I can offer to my community and my neighbors. Even if we don't agree, I want to be a person who can have those conversations and I want to be a person who truly listens.

AR *What inspires you most about the South?* EL I love the seasons, the beautiful trees and landscapes, the mountains, and the sunsets. And I love the food!

AR *How do you think creativity unites us across political, social, and economic divides?* EL I think that no matter who you are or where you live it's important to make friends outside your bubble. Living in a bubble doesn't help you grow.

AR *What drew you to your space?* EL We lucked out to find this 1970s dream home in preserved seventies style. We modernized it to our own taste, but kept the strong seventies bones that drew us to it in the first place. When we designed it, I was inspired by Palm Springs and those mid-century estates, and I think that comes through. But it's also infused with some Southern elements and a lot of extra texture to make it cozy during our long Tennessee winters.

AR *What is your design philosophy?* EL My philosophy is that it's possible to love every detail of your home. Even if the whole renovation is DIY or the whole house is done

RIGHT
The rainbow-colored book collection in her living room took years to compile.

"I WANT TO BE A PERSON WHO TRULY LISTENS."

on a thrift-shopping budget. A home's style is defined by how selective you are when choosing elements, collecting, and renovating—not by your budget. If it's rushed, it will look rushed. You can't rush a collected look. I live by this in my fashion choices too, as well as shopping for my daughters. I try to be picky and only buy things I truly love. I like for the things we own to have stories behind them. And I love to stay within a color scheme I love most, with occasional rainbow moments.

AR *What is your personal color palette?* EL Orange, yellow, and white forever.

AR *The key to making a house a home?* EL All you really need are basic pieces you love, some books, some games, flowers, and coffee. Maybe pizza too.

AR *What makes your space a happy and joyful space?* EL I like the balance of a light and airy vibe—lots of white, minimal decor. And then pops of rainbow and fun accessories, like our seventies-inspired hand chair. I love the Dorothy Draper quote, "I always put in one controversial item. It makes people talk." I try to live by that in my spaces.

AR *What are your daily rituals?* EL Every morning I diffuse essential oils all over my home. Lately I've been liking blood orange, spruce, and grapefruit as my morning blend. I work hard during my work hours and I get lost in playtime with my daughters after that.

AR *What does creativity mean to you?* EL Thinking fresh. It's easy to get stuck doing the same things over and over. I'm always trying to mix it up a bit.

AR *What life pivots have you had either professionally or emotionally?* EL I've failed so many times. We've closed stores, shut down product lines, and pivoted more times than I can remember. It's funny how from the outside, people always see your successes, but what they don't see is all the struggles and uphill climbs.

AR *Best life advice you offer, or best life advice you've received?* EL This advice changed my life forever. I was twenty-six and I owned a struggling local shop, was writing the early days of *A Beautiful Mess*, and could barely pay my bills. My friend who was farther along in his career told me that I needed to set up at least four revenue streams for my business, just like the legs of a table. So if one went away it wouldn't devastate me financially. I took this advice, and just a few years later our business had its first million-dollar year. I still tell it to everyone starting off. One revenue stream, no matter how good it is, is not enough to secure a business, even if one makes a million dollars! Add more until you have at least four.

AR *What is your personal mantra?* EL I only compete with myself and I only do business with people who believe in karma.

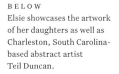

BELOW
Elsie showcases the artwork of her daughters as well as Charleston, South Carolina-based abstract artist Teil Duncan.

"I LOVE IT WHEN PEOPLE
TAKE BIG CHANCES IN THEIR
DESIGNS IN EVERY FORMAT
OF ART. THE WORLD CAN'T BE
ALL VANILLA ICE CREAM."

BIOGRAPHY
—

ALLISON CRAWFORD DESIGN
FOUNDER OF HOTELETTE
VINTAGE DESIGNER

ALLISON CRAWFORD

AUSTIN, TEXAS

"WHEN I GET KNOCKED DOWN, I STAND BACK UP AND MOVE FORWARD FEARLESSLY."

Immediately upon entering one of Allison Crawford's properties in Dallas, Austin, or Nashville, one is immersed in local culture. Not only do her spaces incorporate work from homegrown artists, but they also garner inspiration from the cities themselves. The decor-centric vacation rentals that form her HOTELette empire are located in the up-and-coming hotspots of each locale and effortlessly braid old and new. For instance, her bedroom marries traditional hardwood floors and heavy drapery with unexpected deep plum walls and accents to lend it an outside-the-box playfulness. Allison loves mid-century flea market finds and lots of color and saturation, and she's not afraid to incorporate nuance and kitsch. From vintage records to hot pink walls, her spaces reflect the young, fun demographic that inhabits them. She's fearless in her design approach, evidenced by the bold "love" room (see opposite). The piece of graffiti art reminds us that love is like creativity and comes in a thousand different forms. Allison embraces that and pairs the piece with a sophisticated electric-blue piece of art, a bright yellow pillow, a retro vintage space chair, and a rug sourced from Morocco, and it all works. Like Allison, whose personality is that of a "go-with-the-flow" connector, her spaces organically come together to tell a joyful, happy story of the places she's been, passions she's pursued, and, of course, the things she loves.

—

AR *Tell us about yourself.* AC There are the external, tangible things—entrepreneur, designer, mother—but also the internal, intangible—a love of travel and an interest in mentoring young women.

AR *What ties you to the South?* AC Austin,

Texas, is my chosen home. I was born and raised in Virginia and moved to South Florida at the age of ten. After attending high school in New England, I missed the warmer weather and moved to Dallas to study advertising at Southern Methodist University. With the exception of two years in Manhattan, I've spent my professional years in Texas. I was drawn to Texas because of the friendly people and sense of pride. Austin is a fantastic place to be a female entrepreneur and creative.

AR *What inspires you most about the South?* AC The architecture of Southern cities inspires me: I love the colorful, shotgun homes of New Orleans and the bright art deco buildings of Miami. The South is full of beautiful places, and I'm constantly traveling to those places (and others) for new cultural experiences and interior design inspiration.

AR *How do you think creativity unites us across political, social, and economic divides?* AC Creativity doesn't adhere to political, social, or economic divides—no matter who you are, where you come from, what you believe in, or what you look like, creativity can strike you.

AR *What does the Playful New Southern mean to you and how is this reflected in your home?* AC The Playful New Southern embraces how fun it is to make a space yours, encouraging us to be joyful and playful in a process that is too often overly serious and overthought. To me, it harks back to the idea that if you buy only the things you love, the space will both flow and be a true reflection of your personality and passions.

AR *How did you approach the design of your space?* AC When designing HOTELette, we started by sourcing locally from female entrepreneurs and makers. It is in this initial sourcing experience that we created the mood and feel of the space, although we always prioritize light, comfort, and a spirit of gathering.

AR *What is your favorite light paint color and what is your favorite dark paint color?* **AC** Super White by Benjamin Moore is my go-to white, while Farrow & Ball Railings is my go-to dark paint color. For a dose of femininity, Farrow & Ball Pink Ground is the best pale pink and basically acts as a neutral.

AR *What is your design philosophy?* **AC** My general home-design philosophy is that you must love every individual piece in your home, from the couch to the cushions, to the books, to the art. If you don't love it, don't have it in your home.

AR *What did you have the most fun designing in the space?* **AC** Sourcing art and lighting is my favorite part of the design process. Also, I always try to incorporate vintage into the space, because I love hunting for vintage decor that most people consider junk.

AR *What does creativity mean to you?* **AC** Creativity is the freedom to feel and think with vulnerability and without fear of judgment. I express my creativity through design and developing HOTELette's experiential offerings.

AR *How do you let yourself be vulnerable enough to share your creativity?* **AC** To put it simply, I had to move past caring what others think. In letting go of your interest in others' opinions, you can get in touch with your most creative self.

AR *How do you consider yourself a courageous human?* **AC** I think I've always been naturally resilient and purposeful, although "not taking no for an answer" was a learned skill. When I get knocked down, I stand back up and move forward fearlessly with more purpose and drive.

RIGHT
Farrow & Ball's Brinjal was selected for the bedroom's walls and the custom tabletop for its bold and playful hue. Allison added this tabletop to the giraffe sculptures from Scout Design Studio to make a functional wall console.

BIOGRAPHY

—

AUTHOR OF *WANDERFUL*
WORLD TRAVELER
FUTURE SHAMAN

ANDI
EATON

NASHVILLE, TENNESSEE

Andi Eaton's home tells the story of her life, career paths, personality, and myriad adventures. If you don't know her well, Andi's wittiness and silliness might take some time to uncover, but these traits are instantly apparent in her home choices. From the living room designed entirely around a colorful Bill Murray painting by artist TJ Black (which also happens to be one of the first things she sees in the morning and always makes her smile) to the quirky souvenirs, records, and cameras displayed with abandon, it all adds up to a sense of unbridled self-expression you immediately feel upon entering her space. Her design sensibility centers on inspiration from old architecture (think the weathered colors and patinas of old buildings), and this is evidenced by the worn-down trunks in her bedroom, which set the stage for the room. They were family heirlooms from a great-great aunt who traveled Asia in the thirties. Andi then added rugs she found in Mexico to the walls, and a rack of clothes next to her bed, which serves to bring in yet another layer of color and textiles. Instead of relegating her garments to the confines of a traditional closet, she chose to celebrate the idea that what you put on your body each day should inspire you to fully step into your truth and your worth, and be beautifully displayed.

—

AR *What ties you to the South?* **AE** I've never lived anywhere else. From North Carolina, to Georgia, to Louisiana, and now Tennessee, I've always called a Southern state home.

AR *What does The New Southern mean to you?* **AE** I take after my grandmother Norma Louise—and to me she was the definition of New Southern. She was a transplant to the South—a polished jet-setter with a tropical flair, and she came by it honestly. She spent her summers

traveling, and I love looking back at photos of her in day dresses, a neatly tied bun on top of her head—the top-knot before it was hip—and pearls. Her home was filled with treasures from her adventures. I've adopted both her look and her style philosophies: Invest in meaningful pieces that you will keep forever, things that will remind you of where you've been and who you are—that's what The New Southern means to me.

AR *What inspires you most about the South?* **AE** The sense of home, the ease and laissez-faire attitude, the food, the flora and fauna, the music, poetry, art, and literature. Ah, there's so much!

AR *How do you think creativity unites us across political, social, and economic divides?* **AE** Art is a universal language. I've traveled the world: In the last six months, I've spent time in Southeast Asia, South America, the Caribbean islands, and more—and no matter where you go, creativity is a common language.

AR *How do you see creativity as an important force in today's South, and the country as a whole?* **AE** When I began traveling to research the stories featured in my most recent book, *Wanderful*, a road-trip guide for fashion-forward travelers, it was at the beginning of the 2016 election cycle. I had no idea who I would meet, what stories they would tell, what their struggles and successes might be. What I found was that artistic endeavors united people. Two people could be sitting on completely opposite sides of the political spectrum, for example, but those same two people could sit side by side and listen to music, or stand shoulder to shoulder in an art gallery.

AR *How is the Playful New Southern reflected in your home?* **AE** The word play is one of my core-value words. We all have thoughts,

LEFT
Andi's bedroom nook serves as both personal inspiration and conscious consumption. Vibrant, vintage dresses add a little luxury to Andi's spiritual morning routines.

"CREATIVE EXPRESSION HAPPENS WHEN WE GIVE LIFE TO WHAT ALREADY EXISTS INSIDE."

ideas, emotions, and images bouncing around in our minds—creative expression happens when we give life to what already exists inside. That's what having a playful home is all about to me.

AR *What drew you to your space?*
AE New Orleans will always be home for my boyfriend Ben and me, and the inspiration we each gain from that city is immeasurable—however, Nashville offers so much to the creatives living here. We considered quite a few cities but wanted to be in a place where my boyfriend could make music and where I could take time away to write, while still having the energy of a music-driven city nearby. Our home is walking distance from an old-school downtown square with an old-fashioned soda shop, a theater, a juice shop, and a farmer's market—plus lots of antique shops and locally owned boutiques. It's an easy drive into Nashville, and surrounded by natural areas and parks, so we're able to feel a bit of respite when we're home.

AR *What makes your space a happy and joyful space?* **AE** I'm reminded every time we host friends and family here that it's truly a magical space. I've learned to slow down and not worry so much about creating perfection, and instead to focus on what will create warmth and a glow. For example, when someone visits, I'll send them home with a chakra stone, an essential oil, or an herbal blend that I burn—smell is linked to memory, so it's a way to create lasting memories. That to me creates a joyful space:

when friends or family visit and create memories with us.

AR *What are your daily rituals?*
AE Here's what's on my daily list: a morning Ayurvedic cleansing routine. I cleanse my chakras while cleansing my face, scrape my tongue, and do some deep breathing. I also meditate several times a day. In my bedroom, there's a mini altar on my fireplace mantel—it has crystals, seashells, essential oils, coins, and notes. The altar serves as a place to reconnect to feelings experienced during my travels and steady my mind in moments of overwhelm or stress. It's a sacred and visual reminder of my place out in the world and the experiences I've had. I journal every day too—oftentimes, I spend hours on end writing at the farm table that's situated along the northern window—energetically, it's the heart of the house.

AR *How do you feel when you're creating?*
AE Luxurious, expressive, open.

AR *How are you living your best life right now*? **AE** Presently, I'm leading retreats for creative women, and continuing to share stories on my blog while working on a new book at the same time. My personal mission is to inspire self-worth in women through creativity, holistic living, and experiential travel, and I personally have never felt more settled in my being doing this sort of work. The feelings that women have when they open their hearts—I could not have imagined the gifts it would bring into my life.

ABOVE
Art evokes joy. Proof of this is Andi's playful placement of Louisiana artist TJ Black's Bill Murray painting over the fireplace.

THE COFFEE TABLE IS
THE NEW MANTEL

STYLE

A COMMUNAL SPACE This is your chance to transform traditional concepts of design in your own fresh, new way. The New Southern highlights the beauty in creative and cultural differences within the South and all across the country. Design can connect us to something larger than all of us, and the coffee table can be a first step in cultivating this community-driven approach. By adding substance when styling a space, with an eclectic display of visual elements that all work together, we are reminded that we're always stronger as a whole.

TELLING YOUR STORY The coffee table is also meant to tell a story. It is meant to be an anchor of interaction, rather than being topped with prized possessions that you never touch. It's a spot to showcase new loves, old treasures, and sentimental ornaments. In its replacement of the traditional mantel, it has become the center of a space meant for gathering, a charming vignette to welcome guests not only into your home, but into your life. Here are my three steps to creating a well-curated New Southern coffee table.

—

1. Pick an anchor. Choose an item based on ceiling height and the shape of your surface.

You can go with a low anchor that has a wide surface area or a tall anchor. (Think low and wide for depth or tall and airy for height.) If you are working with ten-foot-high ceilings, you can anchor the coffee table with beautiful branches in a tall vase, and if your space is a little more intimate, you can create an illusion of height with branches or you can add a wide bowl filled with a Monstera leaf or dahlias, as seen in this image. **2.** Stack away. Think in layers using books, bowls, trays, and any sentimental possessions that yield joy. I love to make my stack using either three items or five items. Stacking is the perfect way to incorporate personal elements and conversation starters. As seen in this image, my stack includes a white serving platter with two books, a candle, and my energy-clearing crystal for all the good vibes. Other good stackable ingredients include vintage keys, a collection of matchbooks, heirloom tassels, or even a small oil painting used as a book topper. **3.** Add proof of life. I love homes that look lived in and loved in. On the coffee table, this can be as simple as an open book that someone is reading, textured bone beads I picked up at a flea market when I was shooting on location, or a pair of reading glasses to welcome guests to sit and stay awhile.

CHILDLIKE IS
THE NEW GROWN-UP

SUBSTANCE

How often do we forget to play? As we get older, we place less value on free-flowing experiences and general lighthearted silliness, but these activities are necessary to foster creativity and imagination. As children, we finger paint, draw, build, and explore. These acts of curiosity are intuitive, with less focus on the outcome and more attention on losing yourself in the moment. As adults, I encourage us all to journal, to draw, to take flower-arranging classes, paint pottery, plant an herb garden, cook something messy but delicious, and slow down. We can also jump on a trampoline or go down a water slide, or just look at the sky and name the shapes in the clouds. To live a truly full life, it is necessary to pick the pretty flowers and link arms with a friend and skip somewhere new. Stay curious and weird. It is important never to lose sight of your childlike wonder, and your sense of playing for playing's sake. Run through the sprinkler. Pick up a paint brush. Play with chalk. Sit at a picnic table with friends. Eat a peanut butter and jelly sandwich. Being responsible and being carefree are not mutually exclusive, and playing is not juvenile—it is the stuff from which art and creativity and dreams spring eternally.

PAINT COLORS

USED BY THE NEW SOUTHERNERS

19 – 29

ALYSSA ROSENHECK
STRONG WHITE NO. 001
FARROW & BALL
—

30 – 97
LAID-BACK

ERIN NAPIER
DOVER WHITE 6385
JASPER 6216
SHERWIN-WILLIAMS
RANDOLPH GRAY CW-85
BENJAMIN MOORE

TRACY LORTON SALISBURY
CHINA WHITE PM-20
CHEATING HEART 1617
BENJAMIN MOORE

TAYLOR ANNE BLISS
WHITE DOVE OC-17
METROPOLITAN AF-690
BENJAMIN MOORE
BLACK BLUE NO. 202
FARROW & BALL

RUTHIE LINDSEY
PINK GROUND NO. 202
FARROW & BALL

SHEA MCGEE
SIMPLY WHITE OC-117
MIDNIGHT 2131-20
BENJAMIN MOORE
—

98 – 133
COASTAL

GRAY MALIN
CALAMINE NO. 230
MOLE'S BREATH NO. 276
FARROW & BALL

RAQUEL GARCIA
WEVET NO. 273
FARROW & BALL
SILVERBLADE NO. 7048
FINE PAINTS OF EUROPE

ALLISON CASPER ADAMS
HAGUE BLUE NO. 30
FARROW & BALL
–

134 – 191
COLLECTED

LEANNE FORD
DELICATE WHITE 1001-1
BLACK MAGIC 1001-7
PORTER PAINTS

HOLLY WILLIAMS
DOWN PIPE NO. 26
FARROW & BALL
–

192 – 229
PREPPY

CAITLIN WILSON
DEEP ROYAL 2061-10
BENJAMIN MOORE

GEN SOHR
DELICATE WHITE 518-1
PORTER PAINTS
TRICORN BLACK 6258
SHERWIN-WILLIAMS

HAYLEY MITCHELL
ALL WHITE NO. 2005
OFF-BLACK NO. 57
FARROW & BALL
–

230 – 281
MINIMAL

BROOKE MORGAN
SIENNA DUST PPU3-8
BLACK EVERGREEN MQ6-44
BEHR

CLEA SHEARER
SUPER WHITE PM-1
ONYX 2133-10
BENJAMIN MOORE

ELIZABETH PAPE
ULTRA PURE WHITE 1850
BEHR
–

282 – 315
PLAYFUL

ELSIE LARSON
MARSHMALLOW 7001
PRIVILEGE GREEN 6193
SHERWIN-WILLIAMS

ALLISON CRAWFORD
RAILINGS NO. 31
FARROW & BALL

ANDI EATON
JAMAICAN AQUA 2048-60
BENJAMIN MOORE
INDIA YELLOW NO. 66
FARROW & BALL

INSPIRATION

MORE NEW SOUTHERNERS TO FOLLOW

ALLISON HOLLEY
@APPLEANDOAKNASH

ALLISON MOORER
@1ALLISONMOORER

AMANDA NGUYEN
@AMANDANGOCNGUYEN

AMY SHERALD
@ASHERALD

ANN WILLIAMS
@YEARLYCOMPANY

AVA DUVERNAY
@AVA

BILLY REID
@BILLY_REID

CAMILIA ALVES
@WOMENOFTODAY

CAROLINE HOBBY
@CAROHOBBY

CASSIE KELLEY
@CASSIEMKELLEY

CEDRIC SMITH
@CEDRICSMITHSTUDIO

CLARY COLLECTION
@CLARYCOLLECTION

CLEO WADE
@CLEOWADE

DISCO COWGIRL
@DISCO.COWGIRL

ELISE JOSEPH
@ELISE_JOSEPH

ESTER DEAN
@ESTERDEAN

FORBES + MASTERS
@FORBESMASTERS

JASMINE SWEET
@JASMINEKATRINA

JESSE BODINE
@SCOUTANDNIMBLE

JULIE SOLOMON
@JULSSOLOMON

KACEY MUSGRAVES
@SPACEYKACEY

KATHRYN BERSCHBACK
@BERSCHBACK_DESIGN

LALAH DELIA
@LALAHDELIA

LIBBY CALLAWAY
@THE_CALLAWAY

LILLIANA VAZQUEZ
@LILLIANAVAZQUEZ

LINDSAY RHODES
@LINDSAYRHODESINTERIORS

LOVE & LION
@LOVEANDLION

MALLORY ERVIN
@MALLORYERVIN

MARIE FLANIGAN
@MARIEFLANIGANINTERIORS

MARY LAWLESS LEE
@HAPPILYGREY

MASHAMA BAILEY
@MASHAMABAILEY

MAYKER CREATIVE
@MAYKERCREATIVE

MICKEY GUYTON
@MICKEYGUYTON

NATE GRIFFIN
@KANAKANATE

PAIGE & SMOOT HULL
@THEVINTAGEROUNDTOP

PANACHE DESAI
@PANACHEDESAI

RHIANNON GIDDENS
@RHIANNONGIDDENS

SALT & SUNDRY
@SALTANDSUNDRY

SARA RUFFIN COSTELLO
@SARARUFFINCOSTELLO

SEAN BROCK
@HSEANBROCK

SHAWN JOHNSON EAST
@SHAWNJOHNSON

SHEILA YOUNGBLOOD
@RANCHOPILLOW

ACKNOWLEDGMENTS

THANK YOU

Having a dream quickly results in having a village. These are the people who see your vision, invest in it, bring you candy and coffee as you write, keep you company, and travel with and for you. I wouldn't have been able to do any of it without you.

—

I believe transformation is for the courageous, the bold, and those willing to listen to their stillness. I want to thank my editor Laura Dozier and Abrams for giving me the freedom to be bold, the space to be still, and the opportunity to tell a meaningful story. I am beyond grateful to have experienced this journey with my dream publisher and editor by my side.

And to my fairy godmother and literary agent, Kim Perel. You gave me a gift: You saw me as an artist, you embraced my vision, and you championed this project all the way home. I grew through this process as a writer and as a producer because I had you pushing me. Thank you for being the facilitator of a dream and architect to my words. I love you and thank you.

I owe a huge thank you to all who participated. Time is the ultimate gift, and the way you all welcomed me into your spaces with warmth and love, despite full schedules, new babies, television shows, book launches, and house moves is something I am eternally grateful for.

Beautiful change happens when we believe in a vision greater than ourselves. Tremendous thanks to Sarah Smith, Noelle Panepento, and Nate Griffin for being with me from the very beginning. Sarah, no idea I tell you is too big.

Thank you for being my calm through every single high and low. Noelle, you are one of the hardest-working humans I know, and it has been an honor to grow together. Nate, you are the older brother I never had. Your spirit and support motivate me to be even more courageous, and every time I jump in front of your camera, we are creating another meaningful milestone.

If it were easy, everyone would do it. My team leveled up in a way that I am honored and humbled by, turning the New Southern operation into magic when I needed them most. To Julie Mayo, Lacy Morris, Sarah Bracy Penn, Keturah Davis, Rachel Black, Katherine Owen, Ariana Dickson, and Trevor Tyson—I am beyond grateful to know you and love you all deeply.

The one thing we all need is to be truly seen and loved. To my husband Ben, you have given me the space to be free and to soar the sky. You ground my heart, you are my best friend, and I love you and Meyer more than you know. To Erin, Katie, Amanda, Juliana, and Allison, thank you for being sisters to me and a phone call away with an unconditional ear. And last but not least, to my mother. I know strength because of you, and I trust my intuition because of you. Thank you for your unconditional love, Mom.

And finally, to this community. I poured my heart into this space because I sought to become the love I want to see in this world. I see you, I hear you, I believe in you, and I am forever grateful for you.

EDITOR: LAURA DOZIER

DESIGN: ALEX HUNTING STUDIO

PRODUCTION MANAGER: KATIE GAFFNEY

LIBRARY OF CONGRESS CONTROL NUMBER:
2020931050

ISBN: 978-1-4197-4751-9

EISBN: 978-1-64700-175-9

PRINTED AND BOUND IN CHINA
10987654

ABRAMS BOOKS ARE AVAILABLE AT SPECIAL
DISCOUNTS WHEN PURCHASED IN QUANTITY
FOR PREMIUMS AND PROMOTIONS AS WELL
AS FUNDRAISING OR EDUCATIONAL USE.
SPECIAL EDITIONS CAN ALSO BE CREATED
TO SPECIFICATION. FOR DETAILS, CONTACT
SPECIALSALES@ABRAMSBOOKS.COM OR THE
ADDRESS BELOW.

ABRAMS® IS A REGISTERED TRADEMARK OF
HARRY N. ABRAMS, INC.

ABRAMS The Art of Books
195 Broadway, New York, NY 10007
abramsbooks.com